Balance
The Greatest Chase Ever

Martio Harris

I THANK God for the influences I have had in Him during my time on earth. One of the greatest influences that I have had in Him has been my mother, Marie V. Harris-Jones. She is courageous, bold, and never leans on her own understanding (well, sometimes—LOL). She is truly a queen. My wife, Telisha, and the mother of my children— together we are "T&T, the bomb, baby." She has been my greatest inspiration and partner. I pray that the choices I've made on this journey have influenced them as much as they have influenced me. I have been chasing value, and I found it in Christ. My relationships are my most valuable treasures. I will always honor and cherish the people that Yahweh has partnered me with on this purpose-filled journey. Faith has kept me in a winning position in the Greatest Chase ever. I pray for God's blessings upon everyone, especially those who have taken the time to read these words of encouragement. May my testimony refresh, soothe, and entertain the soul of the reader.

Contents

Foreword vii
Prologue ix
    Mother's Influence ix
    Father's Influence xii
Chapter 1 1
    Chasing The American Dream 1
    Get Rich Or Die Trying! 1
    Principles To Live By 4
    Kingdom Purpose Chase 5
    The Dream Infiltrated The Church 6
Chapter 2 11
    Chasing The Windows To Your Soul. 11
    Are You a REAL RAPPER? 12
    The Twist Of The Game 13
Chapter 3 19
    Chasing The Thoughts In Your Mind 19
    You Have The Tools To Change 21
    May 25th: I Will Never Forget That Day 22
Chapter 4 29
    My Greatest Challenge: Fatherhood 29
Chapter 5 35
    Chasing Favor 35
    Coaching Basketball 37
    The Transition 39

Chapter 6 .... **43**
    What Is My Purpose? 47

Chapter 7 .... **53**
    Chasing Wholeness 53
    Taking The Kingdom Home To Religion 55
    The Fight To Bring Home The Word Of God 55

Chapter 8 .... **59**
    Self-Contained Underwater Breathing Apparatus 59
    Trekking Your Own Path. 61
    Welcome To Arizona 62

Chapter 9 .... **67**
    H-model Relationship 70
    A-model Relationship 71
    Stay Balanced; Keep Your Cool 72

Chapter 10 .... **75**
    Chasing Acceptance 75
    Effects Of Trying To Be Accepted 75
    Find Yourself 76
    The Meeting 77
    She Finally Called Me Back 78
    Meeting The Parents 79
    Impressing The Parents 80

Conclusion **81**

Foreword

I AM HONORED to write this foreword for my son, Tio, as I have been with him throughout most of his journey. Being my firstborn son, I have witnessed his commitment to hearing the voice of the Lord and faithfully serving Him for the majority of his life, as far back as I can remember. Tio faces the challenge of navigating a world where many do not understand his spiritual purpose.

As I read this book, I am inspired by Tio's unwavering dedication to being a man after God's own heart. I say this as someone who believes in God, possesses personal knowledge of His Word, and understands His power. Watching Tio's life unfold and witnessing the deepening love he and his family have for our Savior, Jesus Christ, means the world to me. Through reading this book, you will see how he not only teaches and talks, but also walks the walk of life.

I remember when Tio was just 12 years old, he told me, "Momma, the Lord talks to me." At the time, I didn't fully grasp the significance of his words, thinking it was just child's play. However, as time went on, I saw the truth of it within him. After reading this book, I believe you will understand his hunger to obey God's Word and his unwavering commitment to seeking God's righteousness above the opinions of others. My prayer is that others will also be inspired to seek the Kingdom of God through this book.

With love,
Marie V. Harris-Jones.
Your mama.

Prologue

WHEN I WAS a little snotty-nosed boy running around the streets of Kentucky Ave. in Petersburg, Virginia, I felt like I was a little different from the other children in my neighborhood. My beautiful mother gave birth to me eight days before her sixteenth birthday. My mother was one, if not the only one, of her eight siblings who wanted to go to church every Sunday. One of my fondest and clearest memories of her is when I saw her on television singing in the church choir when I was about three or four years old. In the 1970s, it was unheard of to see a person you knew on that little black and white box that showed a whole other world outside of yours, but nevertheless, there she was. The experience of seeing her worship and sing praises to the Lord just absolutely amazed me. I think it was then that I was filled with the Spirit of God because I remember thinking, "I want to be on that box so everyone can see that I love God more than anything." My father was a handsome seventeen-year-old fellow who was already quite the ladies' man, even at seventeen. The story goes that he was my uncle's best friend and was always around, trying to woo my mother. I was told that my mother was a pretty mean, no-nonsense type of young lady. After months and months of "courting," or what they called chasing a woman and spending time with her, he was able to win her over, and she became his lady. They conceived me, and then the fight with the enemy truly began.

Mother's Influence

Marie Vernette Goode-Butts-Harris-Jones, my wonderful, strong mother, was a woman who, as you can imagine, was born loving the Lord and shouted out to God with a voice of triumph. It was around April 1971 when she missed her menstrual cycle. She had barely learned to be semi-independent. Her mother was still having babies, and now she was a fifteen-year-old pregnant girl who had to tell her mother the truth. In the 1970s, it was not a comfortable experience to face the church and your peers in a lopsided school system. It was one of the most devastating challenges a young black woman could face. Any woman would be devastated as a young pregnant teenager with no husband or financial plan to raise this child. My father was not very responsible; he was only 17 and did not have a father around to show him the proper way to conduct himself as a responsible man.

Being a responsible adult would have been a starting point for young black men in the 1970s. They were fighting to be treated as equal citizens. Drugs, sex, and alcohol became pastimes for black Americans. My father's entire family, including his siblings, succumbed to temptation and were overwhelmed by addiction to one of those soulconsuming substances. One of his sisters dedicated her life to the church and lived a responsible lifestyle. In the country's climate during that era, white, established citizens frowned upon minorities. Separate public property was still being used. It was not uncommon to see a "Whites Only" sign posted on half of the doors.

The public education system shunned teen and adolescent pregnancy. In those days, if you were unfortunately found pregnant, you were not allowed to continue attending public school. My mother was an honor student who had to drop out of high school in the tenth grade. Can you imagine the devastation that a young, developing mind would experience after being an honor student throughout school, only to be told that they could no longer attend school? Many young ladies would have been defeated by such a setback, but not my mom. All it did for her was cause her to view the public school system as a flawed institution. The educational system was set up to teach you how to fit into the status quo. She realized that each race and class of people received a different education. She was wise beyond her years. She realized she could get more value from life by leaving her circumstances. Instead of crying about what the system did to her, she took it upon herself to seek education. The military would educate you on a specific skill based on your understanding and comprehension. If you wanted to serve and become a "Government issue," they would find a way to educate you and put you to work. The school thought that they were protecting the rest of their students by expelling those who defied the moral standards of the time. In reality, they were actually creating welfare recipients and broken homes.

Prologue

My mother has always been great at adjusting to life's peaks and valleys. Instead of turning to the world for answers, my mother chose to run to the church. She had no idea what she was about to encounter there. What she thought would be a place of refuge ended up being a den of wolves. When she went to the church about her pregnancy, they had a solution. They claimed they could resolve the problem for good. They told her that it would be best for her and the baby to abort the fetus, stating that she would be giving it back to God. Once again, my mother was devastated. Can you imagine the fear of a fifteen-year-old girl from a poor environment, trying to figure out what was real and what was fake, being told to abort the baby she had been praying for all her life? That baby was going to be her special gift from God. Nevertheless, she loved the Lord and the church more than anything and wanted to please God and the church, so she attempted to abort her first child twice by taking pills. Both times, she threw up before the drugs could harm me. Wow! But God, the master designer, had a different plan for my mother's life. My mother always told me that she prayed for something of her own. When she was growing up, she had eight siblings with whom she shared everything. Her wardrobe was made up of hand-me-downs from her older sister. Can you imagine the self-esteem of a young lady who never had anything new to wear as a child? You must learn to encourage yourself early when living in such poor socio-economic conditions.

That is why I give her all the respect in the world for her perseverance. Even as a young boy, she never failed to reassure me that God had hand-picked and anointed me. In fact, my mother and I had a supernatural experience with God while I was on the football field. I was on one side of the field, and she was standing on the other side, calling me. I took off running towards her, and the next thing you know, I was floating. I know it seems far-fetched, but she witnessed the same thing. We both looked at each other with amazement. I was a fast child, but that was the first time I ever floated. I keep finding out that "With God, all things are possible." These are a couple of instances that shaped my relationship with the Lord. I would have to say that my mother has been one of, if not the most influential, people in introducing the Lord Jesus Christ into my life.

Father's Influence

LET'S TALK ABOUT my father's influence (or lack thereof) in my life. My father, may he rest in peace, passed away at the ripe age of 37 from complications of the AIDS virus. I did not grow up with him in the household. He was the sixth child of nine as well. When he was young, he was quite the ladies' man. Rumors were that he had two other women pregnant at the same time as my mother. The family background on that side was full of mental illness. My family came to this country practicing a religion called mysticism, which involved kneeling and chanting to call the Spirit of God into the atmosphere. They felt like God came in when they sang songs to Him and worshipped Him wholly. It is said that this is where a portion of modern-day Christianity originated. Some would say that this religion is an introduction to witchcraft, but I believe they were people of faith trying all they knew to get to the God of all. Many views have been held concerning the faith of my father's family. One of my relatives told me a story about a time when they and a couple of friends were at my grandmother's house in the country. They went into a shed they were prohibited from entering, and when they returned home, my great-grandmother knew exactly what had happened, what they had touched, and details she could have never known if she wasn't there. She was rumored to be a witch. However, I received nothing but love from her, so all the stories of witchcraft and black magic left me in awe. I still believe they loved the same God who sent His Son Jesus, but they worshipped in the only way they knew how. One reason I am confident in the power of a living God concerning that side of the family is that they established the first black church in a small town on the outskirts of Petersburg.

My father passed away from complications with HIV at the age of 37. He agreed to get tested for the virus and allow the government to care for his medical and mental health for as long as he was alive. They would also take care of his two children, pay for their education, and give them a lump sum of money when they turned 18. The offer was too much for him to turn down. He sold his soul, and in return, he had a few years of free living. He was so carefree that his nickname could have been "Free Willy," with various interpretations. It was more than a coincidence that the small city of 80,000 people, predominantly black, had the highest rate of the virus. I remember

Prologue

my father being the first person I personally knew with full-blown AIDS. This was in 1988. That experience shaped my idea of "being a rolling stone," like my father. I decided it was better to marry than to burn, and I met my wife at the age of 20; we were married by the age of 21.

I have been on a personal journey to regain power, praise, and passion for the glory of God and His Kingdom and to allow His presence to illuminate my life and the lives of everyone I have the opportunity to impact. My birth was a complicated experience from the start. As I mentioned, my mother was young, uneducated, and poor. She faced scrutiny from everyone she loved for having me. After all the challenges before my birth, I was born in a breech position, which means I was turned upside down. I joke about starting off "ass backward" and having to struggle to get into the right position since I've been on this earth. I spent the first year of my life in the hospital due to breathing issues. I used it as an excuse to sin. You know, we religious folk sometimes have great reasons to hinder our blessings by not walking in the will of God. I have found that any and every excuse is good enough for someone who chooses to prioritize their own will over God's will. The Bible tells us in the book of Romans that there are no excuses, but we were all born with the knowledge of God's existence. Acknowledging Christ as your personal Lord and Savior, and not just believing that God exists, but making choices and living with purpose, balance, and a committed heart and mind to serve the Kingdom of God, will bring about an internal transformation. It has produced something in me that will last for eternity. My spirit has been quickened as if I had the same spirit that was placed upon Bezaleel in Exodus 31:2–5 and 38:39–32. God tells Moses that He called Bezaleel and filled him with the Spirit of God, wisdom, knowledge, and craftsmanship. Bezaleel could devise cunning plans with various resources. He was placed and purposed at a time of transition from the captivity of God's chosen people to redemption and the reclamation of the power that we possess as children of the Most High God.

Take a ride with me as I journey through some of the chronicles and adventures of my life. I will reflect on lifealtering moments and provide supporting scriptures that may help you in your personal situation. I am truly honored that you are willing to accompany me on this journey as we draw closer to God, discover our purpose, and share my testimony. If we can learn to balance being a spirit with a body instead of a body with a spirit, we can live a life that will please God and make Him proud to say, "Well done, My good and faithful servant." You will also discover that you will have favor with others. As followers, we are able to produce what He produced (Luke 2:52).

Chapter 1

Chasing The American Dream

BECOMING A FATHER changed that dream. I realized it when I became a responsible parent. I partnered with my wife, and together, we became responsible for another breathing soul. A beautiful soul with a spirit from God and a human body that carries all the emotions and energy I have experienced in my lifetime. Overnight, I was transformed into a man. I didn't just want a dream; I was determined to create a reality that exceeded anyone's expectations. I immediately prayed to God for wisdom and immersed myself in the Word of God, seeking to be resourceful enough to feed the minds and souls of many people, especially those who feel lost and excluded in America, just as I once did.

My goal was never to be seen as the ideal American successful millionaire; my mission was much greater. I wanted God to receive all the credit for using a simple, unconventional person like me. Despite failing Statistics and dropping out of the University of Arizona with only 25 credits left to receive my bachelor's in business administration, the more spiritually attuned I became, the stronger my beliefs grew. I had become firmly grounded in my faith, and the opinions of others mattered less and less to me. Before, I sought the approval of men, but now I carry the presence of God with me wherever I go. I wanted my children to witness the awe-inspiring God I served. This would bring me favor with both God and people. I surrendered my life completely, dedicating my time and finances to Kingdom-oriented projects. I devoted myself to serving the things I believed would bring joy to the Lord.

Get Rich Or Die Trying!

Why do you want to be rich and successful? Is the money you make meant to take care of yourself or to further the business of the Kingdom of God? In the book of 1 Timothy 6, the Bible instructs us on how to fight the good fight of faith. Growing up, we were taught that there were no rules in a fight. There was no such thing as fighting dirty; you fought only to win. There was no honor or respect for your opponent, and regardless of the outcome, it always ended badly. However, in the realm of spirit and faith, the Bible tells us to fight the good fight of faith (1 Timothy 6:12). In today's world, we need resources to fight that fight and win it with diligence so that we can receive a portion of our reward while we are still here on earth (Hebrews 11:6).

In 1 Timothy 6:17–19, Paul provides instructions on how to use our resources, how to conduct ourselves when we have resources, how to share our resources, and how to ensure a continual flow of resources to us. Doing these things and having them be effective in your life is not rocket science. It can all be captured and achieved by applying certain principles consistently. Let me define a working definition of principles for you: natural laws in the human dimension that are just as real, unchanging, and undeniable to all who come across them. They are natural laws that cannot be broken.

There are times when we seem to struggle with everything in our pursuit of success in life. I believe it's because we try to analyze our relationships in the midst of the worst situations, conversations, or heated debates. We base our ideologies on personal experiences and economic conditions rather than remembering the promises of God. We perpetuate our limited subjective view or opinion of life, making it feel like an unfair, rewinding adventure. It's no wonder there are so many divorced citizens in the Kingdom. We have been conditioned to conform to and abide by the laws of the land. Personally, I try to follow the laws in a reasonable and prudent manner. If I have the opportunity to get something back from the oppressive government structure, I capitalize on every opportunity bestowed upon me. We need to personalize our own roadmap to a destination that aligns with the desires of our hearts because God has made us free.

We have lived in a country, atmosphere, and environment that have utilized false information, witchcraft practices, manipulation, murder, a false Sabbath, and a false religion to control our thoughts and access. We have the best media technology in the world, and through my travels, I have been blessed to encounter people from all walks of life. I now realize more clearly than ever before that American religion is the greatest control mechanism ever created.

Chapter 1

It competes closely with the media, as both bond people in a place where we all have to have faith and exist through generational ancestral traditions and personal beliefs based on experience. You are better off when you are willing to stake your soul on the promises of God. His written Word serves as a handbook of promises to bring Him glory through His chosen people. You may suffer certain levels of persecution, but don't let it make you give up on His promises.

God is faithful to connect you with others if you reach out and don't consider your faith too high to fellowship with fellow saints. You are not alone. In our communities, there are people who remain faithful to God's truths and have not completely conformed to fit into the world around them. You don't have to know everything to believe and be faithful. Starting with a mustard seed of faith, you may experience favor with God and men. Instead of leaping off the bridge alone without proper gear, try bungee jumping first. Both require courage, but one requires full commitment. Keep in mind that someone has likely traveled the same road before and has already explored the territory. They have an objective view that can guide you to your destination expeditiously. They have experienced the trials and triumphs. Lean on those who seem to prosper in Kingdom principles. We need to adopt a Kingdom-purposed agenda and focus more on our Father's business. Sometimes, we don't listen attentively enough to obtain the desired results promptly, but there is always a lesson to be learned (2 Corinthians 7:9–11; 8:9–11). Let's not become too proud to take instruction from others. Individuals who exhibit such behavior end up frustrated because they cannot achieve success. Instead of submitting to corrupt leaders, let's submit to God's chosen leadership. When we go to the polls and cast our votes in the hope that our chosen candidate, whom the government selected for us, wins, our perspective on the whole world changes if our candidate loses. The government selects the candidate, while we get a chance to possibly elect that candidate to be our chosen leader.

When we decide to follow principles that have been written and proven effective for thousands of years, we can avoid much grief and hardship. The anointing that comes from submitting to higher authority will propel your life into another dimension. If we seek wise counsel from those with an objective view of the situation (Proverbs 9), we can accomplish many more goals.

We now have the opportunity to leave a legacy and break free from the curse of slavery, property, and resentment. We were never given the benefit of the doubt. By changing our perspective on what we consume, we can reclaim our rightful positions as God's chosen people. How we perceive our subjective reality serves as our roadmap, leading us to turmoil or a place of peace.

Our mindset may change as circumstances change, but we must continue relying on the Word of God. The goals we have written down and God's plans for our lives should be our guiding lights. They will help us overcome any temptation that distracts us from His holy covenants.

Our individual lenses and perspectives do not alter the existence of objective reality, even though the presence of others may affect that reality from moment to moment (Galatians 2).

This immensely valuable principle of how you view your reality determines how you live and how stable you are on this journey. If you truly achieve success, people will notice. Likewise, if you are truly tumultuous, it will also be evident. The principles you are taught determine whether you grow or disintegrate, whether you build or destroy, and how effectively you live your life. Matthew 6:33 tells us, "Seek ye first the kingdom of heaven, and all these things will be added onto you."

Principles To Live By

These principles must be taught (trained and instructed), implemented (put into force or used), and applied (devoted to a particular use or spread upon) (Deuteronomy 6:6–7). I would like to challenge you to examine some of these principles and define what they mean to you personally (Ron McIntosh, The Greatest Secret).

1. Principle of fairness
2. Principle of integrity
3. Principle of wholeness
4. Principle of potential
5. Principle of service
6. Principle of quality or excellence
7. Principle of fairness
8. Principle of nurturance
9. Principle of encouragement

Chapter 1

Since I learned these principles at the age of 22, I have effectively applied them in my life. I was inspired to let go of religion and the need to always be right. Instead, I accepted the Lord Jesus Christ, the living Messiah, as my King, Lord, and Savior. I understand that money is merely legal tender for trade, and I am aware of the growing presence of Bitcoin in the USA. I am a part of a Kingdom with unlimited resources. For what I don't possess, the King will transfer the wealth of the wicked to meet all my needs. I consider myself to be the richest man on earth. God has blessed my family and me with good health, as we have not experienced any serious illnesses thus far. My children all love and obey the Word of God. They have followed my leadership into the barbering profession and have become licensed instructors, reaching the pinnacle of the profession. They serve their communities and respect others' lifestyles and opinions. They are partners, owners, and managers at our family-owned business, NOBBA Academy (Nation of Barbers and Beauty Academy).

Kingdom Purpose Chase

My dream is Kingdom-purpose-driven. I happen to be born in America, which can be likened to modern-day Egypt and Babylon. Our country, where we physically reside, offers numerous distractions that make it easy to lose focus and have a limited impact for the Kingdom of God. While I may stumble, feel discouraged, or shed a few tears amidst life's obstacles and trials, I choose not to accept limitations. I live a purpose-driven life. I partake of the fruit of righteousness, and when the Lord presents a way of escape, I resist the temptation to seek knowledge in everything and mind my own business. I steer clear of the tree of the knowledge of good and evil, which is how I perceive the American media.

The chase of the American Dream has been a distraction, keeping our focus on worldly gains rather than Kingdom living. Working diligently and consistently in America can indeed provide an amazing lifestyle, if that's all you're seeking. If you make enough money, all your problems will magically disappear, or so it seems. However, many of the wealthy individuals we aspire to be like are spiritually dead. Money has become their master. The false notion and fallacy of joy that money brings will ultimately lead to a premature demise with eternal consequences for one's soul.

The Dream Infiltrated The Church

When I decided to embrace my calling to preach the Gospel, I had no idea I would encounter the level of deception I witnessed within certain church business practices. Some of these practices lacked integrity and mirrored the corrupt practices found in the secular world. They seemed to be just another business entity trying to exploit the American tax codes. The realization began to unfold at my first Mega Church Conference, where T.D. Jakes gathered the most prominent ministers in the Christian community at the Superdome. The conference featured renowned speakers such as Bishops Eddie Long, Juanita Bynum, Paula and Danny White, Jamaal Bryant, and Pastor Tim, as well as guest speakers like Deion Sanders and Ray Lewis.

These men served as both my teachers and contemporaries in the faith, and their influence and anointing were undeniably powerful. The conference theme was "Leading While Bleeding." The anointing I received from God's presence at the conference was like nothing I had ever experienced before. Yet the theme encapsulated the pain and inequity present in their personal lives. The moral of this story is that the activities that most of these people of faith were involved in came from darkness into light. Their faithfulness to their calling was overshadowed by the allure of the American Dream.

Bishop Jakes's daughter became pregnant at the young age of 13. Juanita Bynum had a public physical altercation with her ex-husband, who was also a pastor, leading to a public divorce. Paula and Danny White divorced and later remarried. Additionally, Paula became the personal pastor of the White House during Donald Trump's presidency. Jamaal Bryant's infidelity became known, and Pastor Tim overdosed on drugs in his hotel room. These individuals were meant to set an example for their followers, yet some of them exploited their flock for personal gain. These experiences caused me to reject religion as it was presented to me in America. My personal interactions with local pastors and ministers did not thrive, and I witnessed results in their ministries that I did not wish to replicate.

Chapter 1

Many of them were in their second or third marriages. If a man cannot effectively minister in his own home and foster positive relationships, how can he be qualified to lead a family outside of it? Having traveled to various countries and encountered people from diverse races, backgrounds, and ethnicities, I gained a greater understanding of the manipulation employed by organized governments and the hierarchical structure of the church that controls the masses. They uphold the current power structure, and it is essential for us to resist the temptation to seek such power. The true power of God lies in love, which transcends language barriers effortlessly and effectively.

I have made the conscious choice to love unconditionally in my relationships. I have let go of my selfish desires, instilled by American culture, to pursue wealth, a large house, a white picket fence, and tons of money. In exchange, God has blessed me with unlimited resources to fulfill the calling He has placed on my life. My wife once shared her perspective on the white picket fence with me, expressing that while many spend their lives striving to "get on the other side," she couldn't wait to escape it. To her, it often felt like a form of punishment. She was raised by educated parents who made the most of their resources and provided her with material possessions. They even opened their home to foster children. However, what overshadowed these external attributes was the lack of personal connection within their household. The pursuit of success can drain the love from a relationship. It is widely known that ambition is necessary to achieve a semblance of success in America. Yet, once success is attained, maintaining it over time can lead to significant tension between partners. When the pressures of success dominate one's childhood and adolescence, it's understandable why my wife eagerly sought a life beyond the confines of that white picket fence. In America, there exist two realities. One is shaped by the mass media, while the other is determined by how we choose to utilize our skills, talents, and time. It is crucial to prioritize seeking the Kingdom of God above all else and take responsibility for the reality we create.

Together, we have made the decision to fully embrace one another and construct a meaningful reality. We are dedicated to leaving a lasting legacy and will remain steadfast in this commitment until the return of the Lord.

Balance - The Greatest Chase Ever

Chapter 1

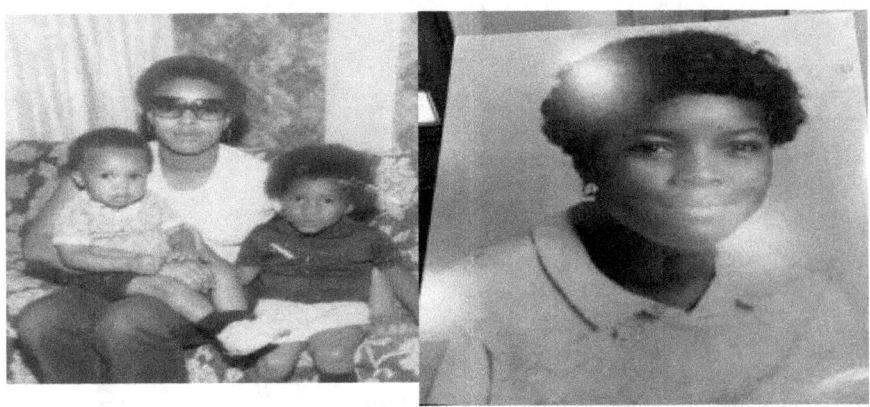

1- William Bitts, Keith, Ronnie (Baby). 2- Dad's siblings 3-Family photo (father-in-law). 4- Mom, dad (Cleve), and me (Frankfurt, Germany). 5- Mom and Plado. 6- Mom, Elvae, and I. 7- Mom at 15 years. 8- Mom military

Original L.A.D.

ROI Crew

Family Tie

T&T the Bomb Crew

Me, Pastor Moss, Lute Olson, Derek Gory (preaching days)

Chapter 2

Chasing The Windows To Your Soul.

KINGDOM GREETINGS, ONCE again beloved in Christ. Recently, I have been reflecting on how well God knows and loves me and how well I truly know Him. How much do I really know Him? The Holy Spirit led me to Psalms 139, where King David prays and reminds God, "Lord, you have searched me through and through and have known me." He goes on to say He knows when we go down and when we rise. He even knows our thoughts and concerns. In John 2:24–25, He states that He sets a pathway for you and covers and protects you when you are asleep. God is very familiar with all of our ways. He knows every word that will roll off of our tongue because He knows our hearts, and out of the abundance of the heart, the mouth speaks (Matthew 12:34). Hebrews 4:13 states that not a creature exists that is concealed from His sight. His love is so deep and intimate that He embraces us and surrounds our whole being if He is allowed to. His hand holds our future and our present. He is a gentleman, so He only moves on our call. He allows us to come to Him boldly (Hebrews 4:16) as long as we are humbled in His presence (Matthew 5). Because He is omniscient (all-knowing), He understands and acknowledges our imperfections, yet He loves us even more when we repent.

Let us take a moment to remember the story of the Prodigal Son. That is an excellent illustration of trying to accomplish what God has for you on your own timeline. The parable shows a son who strays and returns to his father. When his son returns home, the father rejoices and sets a king's feast for him. That is how God rejoices when one of His own comes home. We can barely understand that parable without looking at it with humility. Someone may respond after that parable with, "Are you telling me that if I experience a sinful lifestyle, I am still a candidate for an inheritance from God?" Yes, if you repent. Thank God for Jesus.

The Bible tells us that Jesus came for the lost (Matthew 15:24). "So are you saying if I try to live a perfect life, I don't get rewarded?" No, what I am saying is that if your perfection is of your own works, your perfect life still ends in eternal failure (1 John 2:4).

We cannot hide from the truth because the Spirit of truth, which is the Holy Spirit, which is God, still moves among the faces of the deep (Genesis 1:2). God even holds the keys to death and hell (Revelations 1:18). If we let Him lead us, He already has a beaten path so that all that happens to us will be good (all things work for the good of those who love the Lord). So we can stop doubting any good thing if we love God and believe His Word is true. He ordained your life while you were yet a mere concept and blessed you for an expected birth in your mother's womb (Jeremiah 29:11). God thought about you extensively before He delivered you to this earth; He designed you for a specific purpose, gave you a specific plan or path, and established a specific destiny for you. Seek Him diligently, and you will be rewarded in this life and in eternity (Hebrews 10:35; 11:6).

What is the truth? What is my truth? What do you really believe deep down in your soul? These are the questions that I wrestle with daily. I have this struggle because of how religion was introduced and taught to me. I always felt like the gospel was taught in an oppressive manner. I realized it was good news for some but calamity and suffering for others. Most of the time, the way that it was taught by my leaders, teachers, and parents didn't seem to produce supernatural results. While we were singing and chanting about overcoming, whenever I visited a predominantly Caucasian church, Xit seemed they were experiencing more victory. I felt that the gospel was used as a restrictive tool to constrict the progress of the black race. The way it was taught to me and the way that I received it did not give me a wealth of knowledge and understanding. I still took my family religiously to service every Sunday. I did not believe it was the Sabbath, yet I observed it anyway. I was afraid I would not be aligned to receive the American dream everyone was chasing.

Are You a REAL RAPPER?

One of the main reasons I lived was to become a rapper. I believed that by mastering my craft, I could achieve fame and live the American dream. However, this pursuit turned out to be a nightmare. When I finally woke up from this chase and allowed my true purpose to be realized, I became more effective in serving God.

The Twist Of The Game

    I had a love for the entertainment industry that was insatiable. I was fascinated by its influence. It offered the opportunity to reach a large number of people with my gifts and talents, and I had a chance to make a lot of money. Game and money—who can deny that? It seemed as though that was the answer to all my worries. My younger brothers Elvae, Plado, and our best friend Rise (Juan), whom we consider a brother, came together to make some great music. Our mutual enthusiasm for the rap game was contagious. We formed a rap group in 1993. It was initially known as L.A.D., which stood for "Living a Dream" or, jokingly, "Light Another Doobie." My brothers Elvae and Juan began performing together as L.A.D. before I joined them. They had a musical style reminiscent of the popular group Bone Thugs-n-Harmony. I was initially just a fan of L.A.D., and after watching from the sidelines, I got involved with the business side of the industry. We were not progressing fast enough for me, so I decided to join the group as a member to try to bring some hype.

    One missing element in our group was a hypeman, and I fit that role perfectly. I had a knack for shifting the atmosphere and making a lasting impression. My rap name was Crazy Marty, and I played my part with precision. I juggled being a businessman, a husband, a father, and a rapper fearlessly. I was willing to take risks and perform acrobatics that most people wouldn't dare. For instance, I once jumped off stage in the middle of a concert performance, landing among thousands of fans. Ice Cube was the headliner. Many of my outrageous actions happened spontaneously, as I instinctively protected those around me. It was my duty to ensure our safety and well-being. This incident wasn't a one-time occurrence; it became part of our modus operandi. During this particular show, unbeknownst to me, one or two of my friends threw up gang signs, even though we weren't associated with any gang. This action provoked an irate individual in the crowd, who shouted something disrespectful at me, possibly saying, "F*** you." The room seemed to fall silent. After gathering myself, I calculated my jump and leaped into action. I launched myself off the stage, executing a Bruce Lee karate kick with the ease of a seasoned Kung Fu practitioner. I believe I soared over ten rows of the crowd. In that moment, I fully embraced my Crazy Marty persona, perceiving a threat against my family and responding accordingly. The concert abruptly came to an end as a massive brawl erupted, prompting the Tucson police department to raid the venue and shut it down.

After that show, we started gaining a negative reputation due to incidents like that one and others I will share later. My passion for music ran deep, almost like a blood tie. I was willing to sacrifice my soul to reach the level of success I believed we needed to achieve. That was one of the few occasions when God gave me the opportunity to live again. Once I realized I was chosen to do His work, I prioritized music and the entertainment industry over representing God's Kingdom. I compromised some of my core beliefs in my verses, fearing I would appear uncool or out of touch. Most people didn't know that I was afraid of public speaking, but most did recognize that my mouth was sloppy. I performed whenever I spoke to avoid slurring my words because I found that performing allowed me to convey my message more clearly. In my youth, I was more willing to compromise my personal convictions for music. For the most part, I believed what I said, and I said what I believed. Some words were very provocative when I said them and produced significant results. That was one of the incidents that occurred before the birth of my children. I am covered with the blood of God. The stronghold that the business carries is death-defying. You are constantly making life-and-death decisions. Yet all of us are still alive.

As success in the world deepened, the sacrifices of my spiritual self became less Holy Spirit-filled. The atmosphere encouraged fulfilling our fleshly desires. Another test came when we went on tour with renowned musicians and major artists from around the world. In our minds, this was the moment. We would have the opportunity to be introduced to a major record company. This was a major breakthrough; if we performed well, we would finally reach our lifetime goal.

My team and I flew out to California and performed all night until our hands and lungs were sore. But as usual, I felt disappointed. I slipped away by myself and engaged in some "Crazy Marty business,"

Chapter 2

which usually involved making some extra money, but this time, I found myself caught up in a situation that could have altered my life forever. There was a tie that was made that should not have been made.

I received a warning from Yahweh in the spirit. His Spirit spoke to me and cautioned me about the potential cost of my continued disobedience. I was urged to be careful not to sacrifice my seed, and the fear of facing Yahweh's wrath made me tremble inside. The following day, my wife surprised me with the wonderful news that we were expecting twin boys. I was filled with excitement but also consumed by the fear that my selfish decisions might jeopardize one of their lives. The pregnancy progressed well for the first few months, and we were expected to have a Csection and a preplanned birth. Our primary care physician had scheduled us for this moment months in advance. In my life, adventure always finds a way to creep in. Surprise, surprise, the day my wife went into labor, we discovered that our primary care physician was on vacation. Panic started to set in, and I couldn't help but think, "What a coincidence, God." The new doctor decided that we should proceed with a vaginal delivery. Unfortunately, complications arose during the delivery. While my wife successfully delivered the first baby, her uterus contracted during the delivery of the second baby, leaving the baby's head halfway outside. The second baby was delivered without breathing. In that moment, I entered into prayer mode and remained calm. I knew that God would not forget my voice. As I released His promises into the universe, the atmosphere shifted. It brought peace to my wife, and God reassured her that everything would be alright. The doctor instructed me to turn off the camera, and we immediately engaged in prayer. I pleaded with God to spare His child, promising to give the baby back to Him. In fact, I promised that I would totally commit my heart to Him. After three minutes of being stillborn and our prayers, the baby miraculously came back to life with a healthy cry. He began breathing normally after a couple of minutes. By the grace of God, he has grown up to be a healthy, talented, and God-fearing young Kingdom builder. I have dedicated all three of my children to God.

I encountered numerous compromising situations due to my involvement in hip-hop. The demands of maintaining social status took a toll on every aspect of my life. It's a struggle, and it's all on

God. The ultimate goal for any musician is fame, to have their music heard and recognized by everyone. My involvement in the entertainment industry led me to encounters with law enforcement at various levels—federal, state, and city. I engaged in high-speed chases, including one involving the late Grammy awardwinning artist DMX (rest in peace), whom I picked up with his manager.

I had the opportunity to share and pray with DMX. I had to strong-arm a club that J. Prince was performing. The promoter used my money to fund a concert, so it became my concert. My team and I flew to Texas and rented a U-Haul. We tracked down the individual who tried to steal my money and made him load all valuable items onto the U-Haul. We then went to the concert venue and collected all the proceeds. We had men stationed outside, I handled the money collection, and a friend ensured cooperation. Scarface was the headliner, and our artist performed before him, so we had to be prepared. I took care of business and paid off potential troublemakers. The remaining artists chased us (at high speed) to the airport. I had approximately $20,000 strapped to my waist from the profits. In the rush and haste of the moment, I left my identification at the hotel room we had rented. When I arrived at the airport, I kept quiet about my mistake and acted as though everything would work out. Surprisingly, the security checkpoint was light, likely because we were rushing and the last to arrive for the latenight Red Eye flight. Once again, I called upon God to bless our journey home. My prayers were answered when the guard noticed the money around my waist. He called me to his line and waved me through the checkpoint. That incident terrified me, and as soon as the airplane took off, my body went into convulsions and tremors.

In my adolescent years, I tried to imitate Nino Brown, a character played by Wesley Snipes, in the gangster movie "New Jack City." I once felt invincible. I was stopped by law enforcement with drugs in my car on a few occasions, and each time Yahweh delivered me from the potential grave. I foolishly took for granted that I was chosen to do God's work and fulfill His will. I should have recognized that it was God's grace and mercy that had protected me all along. The hold that the industry had over me was paralyzing to most, but because of my love for God, I repented and surrendered my life to Him. And you can do the same.

Chapter 2

MadLad Universe 2022

Martio Jr. Lyric, Vae 1998

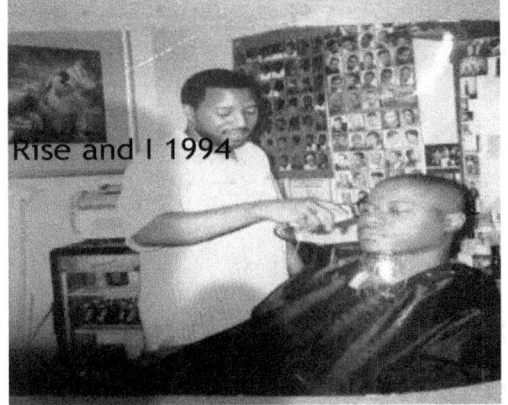

Rise and I 1994

The ROI Team
1993

Twins Graduation
2019

Me (11), Vae (9), and
Plado (4)
1981

Chapter 3

Chasing The Thoughts In Your Mind

AS WE CONTINUE on our journey toward balance, I extend my humble greetings to my readers. You are the chosen children of God. I assume that you have been awakened and are in your right mind. Hopefully, you are filled with the spirit of truth on this day. Let us remember the promises of Yahweh and strive to be in the mindset and spirit of truth. Yahweh (God) is a Spirit, and His Word commands us to worship Him in spirit and in truth (John 4:24). When we worship Him in this manner, our hearts and souls open up to receive the Spirit of Yahweh. Our hearts begin to transform, even if our minds may still hold onto old memories. Sometimes, contemplating past experiences in relationships can hinder us from seeing the incredible future that awaits us. Our focus may become fixed on what we have observed through others. Perhaps you have experienced hurt in the church and been offended by someone. Nevertheless, we must press on toward the higher calling. Instead of depending on the Word of God, we allow our minds to wander. You may ask yourself, "Why doesn't this Gospel seem to work for me?" Your spirit resounds, "I LOVE THE LORD GOD WITH ALL MY HEART." Yet, your prayers and supplications may feel insufficient to move mountains. You are barely surviving and struggling to meet your obligations. You find it difficult to complete tasks, and heartbreaking situations seem to be a constant occurrence. When life becomes an arduous process that constantly disappoints us, our faith is truly tested. We may reach a point where we question God, wondering, "If God is real, then why?" Our faith falters, and we begin to question the very existence of God and the authority He holds over our souls and eternity. Life appears to be regressing, while the wealthiest individuals seem to believe that God is on their side. We desire to become like them and envy their material wealth rather than glorify God through our purpose. As a society, we eagerly chase success and worldly prosperity, often sacrificing everything else we claim to love. You may find yourself on the brink of divorce, considering quitting your job, or even battling suicidal or homicidal thoughts. You feel lost and unsure of what to do or think. All of this pursuit for fame and fortune. It is in these moments that Yahweh must intervene on your behalf. When our minds become distracted and we struggle to focus on purposeful actions, it is a sign that we are out of alignment, beloved. The Bible tells us in Matthew 6:33 to seek first the kingdom of heaven and His righteousness, to align ourselves with the Word and will of God, and all these things will be added unto us. Let's break it down in simpler terms. Yahweh is telling us that if we accept Him in our hearts and allow our hearts to guide our minds, we will have the power we need on this journey to accomplish all things (Philippians 4:19). I understand that you may be thinking, "That sounds good, but it's easier said than done." I will share a few ideas, backed by great philosophers, scientific studies, and hypotheses, that can help us effectively renew our minds (Romans 12:2).

Renewing your mind goes beyond simply memorizing the truth and repeating it when problems arise. It involves transforming your entire decision-making process. It means making heartfelt decisions (with a heart that is full of the love of God) and repeating that process consistently until you have the mind of Christ about that situation. There are various laws or principles that govern success in this world, such as capacity, control, belief, expectation, attraction, correspondence, entropy, cause and effect, hysteria, and motion (as described by Ron McIntosh in "The Greatest Secret"). For the purpose of renewing and regenerating your mind, we will focus on the law of "capacity." This law states that a person can only receive from God in direct proportion to their capacity to receive from God.

Let's consider it this way: If a cup is already filled with stuff, how much more can you pour into it? If the dominating thoughts in your mind are shaped by your past experiences, how can you fully receive God's thoughts without randomly applying His Word only when convenient? Pouring more substance into a full cup will only cause spillage. Instead, commit yourself with an open mind to being re-established. Being a willing vessel for new substance will result in a tremendous overflow of blessings and resources. It requires breaking free from years of false teachings that have shaped the organizational structure of evangelical churches, which often seek to control and manipulate through their interpretation of the Bible. You are now at a stage in your life where the truth really matters. Embrace the truth delivered in love and correction, for it will set you free. Beware of engaging in rhetorical and religious activities that can enslave your soul. Relax your mind and allow your consciousness to expand freely. Think with the heart of God and rid yourself of your "stinking thinking."

You Have The Tools To Change

Changing your mind is much easier than changing your mindset. When an idea is merely implanted in your mind, you can divert from that way of thinking with mental effort. However, when a thought or idea becomes deeply embedded in your mind, it becomes incredibly challenging to reprogram your mindset. Let's consider a childhood example: When we were young, one of the first actions that we naturally took was lying. We lied based on our first experiences because we didn't want people to be uncomfortable with us. One of our most natural actions as humans is the excretion of waste from the body. When a child sees how disgusted we are when they do that act, we frown and say that it is nasty, and we don't want to change the dirty diapers. Their reaction will be to say that they didn't excrete on themselves, so that we don't make them feel uncomfortable. It was a natural, learned behavior; reactions to natural behavior, favorable or unfavorable, are factors related to your social growth. How you perform in a corporate environment indirectly reflects your experiences in early childhood and adolescence. They can damage your ability to be comfortable being yourself, especially when those character traits are taught and continually developed, especially at a young age.

In my family, I was brought up to be a "manly man." The men in my family do not cry. We were taught to have multiple women; in fact, if you didn't have more than one, you were considered less of a man. We were justified by how many women we could have babies with. We weren't taught the importance of raising a child. That crazy mindset carries over into adulthood if you don't catch it early.

Let's explore another instance where Yahweh delivered me from another potential disaster in my life. After not pursuing a professional sports career, I contemplated becoming involved in drug trafficking. I was involved with "friends" that had major hookups. They had front seats with the Mexican cartel. I figured I was smart enough to get away with it as long as I stayed under the radar. I made a fortune after I did a few loads, counting hundreds of thousands of dollars. I traveled across the country each week for deliveries, trying to emulate the character Nino Brown from the movie New Jack City. Eventually, the business became too hot, and I realized I had accomplished everything I wanted in that world. I decided to end the partnership, but my partner asked me to do one last shipment. My fleshly desires and "stinking thinking" led me to accept that final transaction against better judgment. However, Yahweh had a different plan, and this is how I recall the day my brothers and I refer to as "May 25th."

May 25th: I Will Never Forget That Day

The night before the police raid, the atmosphere felt thick and dreary. While speaking to a family member on the East Coast, we sensed that our conversation was being eavesdropped on. We heard strange noises and clicks. My intuition told me this was bad news. Despite the unsettling feeling, I proceeded with our plans. There was a significant amount of money at stake in this drop, so we "prayed" that we were just tripping. After a restless sleep, I woke up the next day, ready to go to the studio. We were putting the finishing touches on a song we were working on, using the money we had earned to pay for the studio time. Following my usual morning routine, I went to the safe and counted out $80,000 in cash. I felt on top of the world. My fellas and I celebrated by jumping around and smoking a blunt, and then we headed to the car. Once everyone was ready, we lit another blunt for the ride and set off.

    As I pulled out of my driveway, I noticed a pickup truck parked across the street with a suspicious-looking man inside, staring at me. I had a strange feeling something was off, but I continued driving. I soon realized that someone was following me. Glancing through my rearview mirror, I saw the pickup truck tailing me. I tried to lose them by taking quick turns and maneuvers, but I couldn't shake them off. To my surprise, a fleet of unmarked undercover police

Chapter 3

vehicles appeared, signaling me to pull over. I prepared my license and registration, trying to remain calm. However, my calmness was short-lived when the police officers donned masks and started closing in on my vehicle.

Fearing for our lives, I accelerated, and the chase began. The pursuit started in the car but ended with them chasing me on foot. I ran past their vehicles and glanced back to see at least 20 police officers pursuing me. During the chase, I navigated through every backstreet I knew, desperately trying to escape. After what felt like an eternity—approximately 20 minutes of a high-speed car chase through Tucson's backstreet neighborhoods—I found myself cornered in a cul-de-sac. My brother, Rise, and I quickly exited the vehicle, leaving $80,000 behind. I was struck on the head with a "Billy Club," causing my head to hit the roof of a nearby house. It felt like a scene from a horror movie. I was bleeding profusely from a split skull; you could see my brain. Despite my dire condition, my primary concern was losing my life savings. I ran until I had nowhere else to go and ended up at a dam behind an apartment complex owned by one of my best friends. I jumped over the dam with the little strength that I had left. Yahweh never fails me. This friend happened to be a registered nurse and had the necessary supplies to bandage my wound temporarily. He effectively patched me up to prevent me from passing out. He then smuggled me in the back of his trunk across the city, taking me to another friend's house. This friend happened to be a quadriplegic with open wounds, but they were able to provide further care for my injury. I called my mother and relatives to let them know I was alive. They had been worried as the high-speed chase and drug bust had made national news headlines.

After about a week on the run, a family friend referred me to a great attorney. She called the appropriate authorities and helped me turn myself in. However, I never had to go through with it. God had a different plan for me to minister outside of prison. He intervened and prevented my arrest, sparing me from going to court or appearing before a judge. During this critical time, my relationship with my father-inlaw, who happened to be a Judge, flourished. He made the decision to retire so that I wouldn't have to face jail time and could receive legal guidance if needed.

That event was life-altering and forever changed the course of my destiny. We were all in danger of being killed by the police. This was not too long after the Rodney King verdict. We were down, but we were not out. I rented one apartment for my wife and another for my brothers. I put everything in my name since I was the only one with credit. We decided to work together to rebuild what we had lost. All five of us, including my wife, applied for jobs at VNU Operations Services, a telecommunications company that took inbound and outbound calls. We all did well working there. At that time, we had a friend who was being investigated for murder and on the run. We referred to him as Scatterbrain. The day after the police raid, he disappeared suddenly and resurfaced 27 years later after serving time in prison. We attempted to release another album as a way to recover from losing everything we had worked for. Juan Spencer joined the military after his wife brought trouble into his life. He struggled to adapt and ended up going AWOL. We had to turn him back into the Army, and although he spent some time in Leavenworth, he is now back with the family. He is the most vocal of the brothers and someone you'd want on your side in a fight. He may come across as stern, but he genuinely loves his family and friends. If you're not part of that inner circle, you may have a difficult relationship with him, or vice versa. I know I can always count on him to have my back, and he expects and knows the same.

My brother Vae is a natural genius who captivates audiences with his versatile and adaptable vibe. He is the main reason I continue making music. His musical talent is so exceptional that it inspires our bandmates to bring their best material. We have created a lot of great music together. I helped produce his best solo album, and he contributed to my Gospel solo album, which was a gift from the Most High Yahweh. However, he eventually decided to move to Texas with his family. We recorded a video at Mount Calvary Church, showcasing his transformation as a changed man. He had dabbled with controlled substances, and his inside joke was that as long as drugs were available, he didn't have a problem. While he found it hilarious, I knew he was speaking the truth. His family moved to Texas due to his lifestyle and the industry. Fortunately, I had the opportunity to record that anointed solo album with him before he left. Over the years, we have built an extensive music portfolio.

My youngest brother, J.R. or Plado, as he named himself when he moved in with me during his 10th grade, became my legal ward so that he could finish high school at Amphi High. Vae completed his education, but Plado didn't. He was too brilliant to pay attention to the public education system. He challenged the teachers all the way up to the 10th grade and told them where they could go. He had plenty of reasons to rebel due to my mother and stepfather's separation. As he grew into his calling and anointing, he used that same "you can't tell me anything" attitude to create a comfortable middle-class lifestyle with his wife, Elisha. He is now my business partner in a couple of ventures and provides all my computer and technical support.

Although we have each embarked on different journeys, we still love, enjoy, and respect one another. We have redirected our talents to glorify the Kingdom, and 25 years later, we released another record together. Our music sounds great, but it also reflects the significant growth and lack of growth in our personal lives. Nevertheless, "MadLad" is forever tattooed on my arm—it's my only tattoo.

In sharing this story, I hope to shift the mindset of the carnal man. The carnal man believes that indulging in just one more sin won't do much harm, and he promises to stop after that. Without renewing our minds and experiencing a complete transformation, it's nearly impossible to break free on our own. We must adopt the mind of Christ Jesus, where everything becomes new and the old gradually fades away. Ask yourself: Are you ready for a new life filled with joy, courage, love, peace, wisdom, and understanding? Start today by renewing your relationship with the Lord. Great minds think of great ideas and use wisdom to impact and inspire others. You have the tools to change. Make up your mind.
Change your destiny.

Family

NOBBA (United Tucson) certification

Chapter 3

NOBBA (United Tucson) certification

NOBBA Phoenix (certification)

Chapter 4

My Greatest Challenge: Fatherhood

IF YOU ASKED me about the greatest challenge in my life, I would say it was raising my three children to be children God would be proud of. I consider myself extremely blessed because God allowed my wife and me to raise these beautiful, handsome, loving, giving, and God-fearing Kingdom-minded gentlemen. Let me share a bit about my oldest son, Martio Junior. Before he was born, I prayed that I wouldn't be the one to mess up his life, so I entrusted him to God. I also prayed to be the kind of father I wished I had. On April 20, 1998, God gave me the challenge of trying to produce like Him before my son. During that time, I was involved in trafficking marijuana across states, from Arizona to Virginia. It was a profitable business for a few months until I faced a potential drug kingpin charge, which never made it to court thanks to the sacrifice of my father-in-law. With so much mercy and grace from God and support from my friends and family, I didn't want to take the gift of a child for granted. I gave up all my worldly thoughts, activities, and possessions. Actually, they were taken by the DEA. I allowed the Holy Spirit to enter my heart the day after an encounter with the law. When the Holy Spirit came in, I experienced intense barking and vomiting for half the night. When I finally regained consciousness, I produced a ninesong gospel album. This album was dedicated to God, my children, and my family. Now, let's focus on Martio Jr. He is a brilliant young man who loves competition, not just to win or claim he's the best, but to genuinely be the best in everything he does. He allowed the Holy Spirit to come into his life at a young age, so my wife and I never faced any major issues with him. He consistently achieved excellent grades throughout elementary, middle, and high school. College presented some challenges for him as his focus shifted to becoming an adult rather than pursuing higher education. Understanding my children's mindset was easier because they are a product of me, my wife, and God. My DNA is in there, and I can only focus on things that genuinely interest me. Therefore, I decided to establish a lifestyle that would create a legacy, allowing them to observe and emulate my actions throughout their lifetime. They are better versions of me and can excel even further.

Martio excelled as a young athlete, outworking everyone on every team each year. While he may not have been the most athletic, strongest, or fastest, he refused to let anyone outwork him. His attitude, coupled with his commitment to the Holy Spirit, has paved the way for success. He found a wonderful wife who also deeply loves the Lord. They are currently expecting their first child. I felt a sense of success when he found the love of his life. My main concern was that they would grow up following God rather than the ways of the world. God showed me favor when it came to my children. I was incredibly blessed when God gave me my second child, but it turned out to be twins, so I have three children. My obedience during my first shower resulted in a double portion. My first conceived twin was Demari. Tomari thought he should have been first, so he's been competing for that position since their conception. It was almost like the story of Jacob and Esau, but as a parent, I tried my best to buffer their competitive spirit when it came to each other. I only got upset with them when they fought or hurt each other.

Demari is the more loving and compassionate of the two. He acknowledges that it can sometimes be seen as a weakness because he allows things to happen until he gets upset, making him appear as a whiner or crybaby. Communication has always been a challenge with him, particularly when I try to correct him. But I understand that it stems from his desire to avoid causing problems and prove his worth as a young king in God's Kingdom. He is a very athletic young man, perhaps the most athletic among the three. Unfortunately, his attitude sometimes hindered his full potential as an athlete. During his childhood, I gave him space to develop into the person he wanted to become while also guiding him to become who God intended him to be. Despite his occasional communication struggles, he has always represented his family and God positively in the world.

Tomari, on the other hand, is very assertive. He has a strong sense of ownership and will not let anything be taken away from him. He demands what is rightfully his. He doesn't display humility when it comes to being the best, and in most activities he participates in, he is considered the top player or the smartest. He acts as the protector of the two brothers and sometimes tries to bully his brother, knowing he loves him. They have chosen God over the world. By the grace of God, my three children have become exactly what I prayed for, even before they were in their mother's womb. Through songs, dances, and a lifestyle of righteousness, I whispered the Word of God into their spirits. I sometimes get into trouble for bragging about watching my seeds grow and seeing how they represent what goes on in our household. I firmly believe you cannot produce bad seeds if you show them the right things and follow the Word of God to fulfill His will. As a parent, it is crucial to provide cover and protection from the world and those who may have more influence on their lives than you do. It is a challenging task, especially when you have to work and may not have as much time as my wife and I have been fortunate to have. However, I consider it a sacrifice well worth making, one that I would make over and over again.

As a young black father, I was determined not to let the world raise my children or influence them more than I did. I didn't have a father figure to guide me. Although my stepfather was in my household for nine years during my adolescence, we never truly connected as father and son, and he never provided me with the necessary discipline. I probably learned more about what not to do as a husband rather than what to do. This experience motivated me to work harder on my marriage and every other relationship. Sometimes, I would step back from my children or my beautiful wife when they challenged my position in order to protect our precious relationship. I would sometimes be assertive in making a point, and once I made it, they could attest to its effectiveness. God will not let you down if you invest the time and effort in your children that you put into making money and pursuing success. He allowed my family to have a successful haircut ministry, providing us with the necessary resources to navigate life successfully without unfulfilled desires or wants. However, I will have to wait and see how my children raise their own children to truly assess how well my wife and I nurtured the seeds God gave and blessed us with. We may have given them years of poor verbal communication that could potentially affect their future relationships, but I pray for God's grace to break that curse. Overall, I am extremely grateful for what God has given me, the responsibility entrusted to me, and the positive outcomes that have resulted.

Chapter 4

Chapter 5

Chasing Favor

"FAVOR FOLLOWS ME" – That was the thought that crossed my mind as I woke up this morning. I rejoice with resounding joy, knowing that the Lord is working for my good. Bishop Demetrius Miles, my ministry partner and pastor of Tucson Church International, would always remind us of this truth, and it's a phrase worth holding onto. I grew up with little to no chance of being successful, so my mind could easily have been corrupted. At least, that was what I was taught. Even with those kinds of odds against me, I have never experienced lack, and for that, I praise God. I praise God that I was raised by a mother who was willing to step out on faith. Her courage caused her to leave her home at the age of 17 to join the military. She made that sacrifice to give her children a better life and protect them from the drug-infested and immoral environment we lived in. The poverty rate was so high that the success rate was just about 2%, and one of the 2% was always the drug dealers. The means by which they obtained their success shouldn't even count. The chances of success seem unattainable for most young African Americans, with the absence of men or leaders in about 60% of African American households. In the U.S., history presents the emasculation of the black man. The standard for him is set so low in the household that it has no consistency and no real measuring point. The fabric of family structure has been torn into bits in most African American heritages and races. These facts have a great impact on how we view and perceive our culture. It reflects how we view our opportunities. We often fail to see the opportunities because our view is distorted by our broken history. We must break the chains of the history that we were taught. To be victorious, we must live God's story and glorify Him. We have to change our perspective. Philippians 3:15–16 states, "Let us therefore, as many as be perfect, be thus minded: and if in any thing ye be otherwise minded, God shall reveal even this unto you. Nevertheless, whereto we have already attained, let us walk by the same rule, let us mind the same thing." One of the secrets to breaking the chains that distort your faith is to press towards a mark of a higher calling (standard) for the prize of the high calling of God in Christ Jesus (Philippians 3:14). You must walk in this new truth and greater perspective, being diligent and intentional with what you have already attained. Yahweh has set the standard for those who follow Him. Paul tells us in Philippians 3:17 to "follow my example and observe those who live after the pattern we have set for you."

As we live in Christ, we should be growing in Christ. By the leading of the Holy Spirit, we should know the correct path. We should be vessels of purpose. The Holy Spirit leads you into all truth. The truth will stretch your capacity. It will propel you further than your reality could ever imagine. We have to try to enjoy God's chafing while He is stretching our capacity. Have you ever questioned which truth is altering your reality? How do you step into the next dimension that everyone speaks of? Embrace the process, understanding that there may be missing information that others know and you have yet to discover. While you are learning to be a king, don't beat yourself up for not grasping all the truth at once. Hold tightly to the truth, and it will set you free.

The Kingdom of God holds the truth you seek. It is fully equipped to provide sufficiency for believers. Yahweh continually reveals the mysteries of His Kingdom (Matthew 4:11), forging a relationship that pushes you out of your comfort zone. As you walk this faith journey in the Kingdom, it is important to have allies. Be aware, for the enemy of Yahweh's people preys on your destiny.

Favor is something I never had to chase; I was born with it. From the moment I entered the world, with Yahweh living in me, I felt like God's chosen son. While I knew I wasn't Jesus, I understood my significant role in bringing forth His Kingdom message to the people. Despite engaging in actions that should have led to serious trouble, imprisonment, or even death, Yahweh's favor always covered me. I recognized the advantage I had been given, and I never took it for granted. There were times when I tempted God's vengeance with premeditated sin, but I quickly repented when I realized my error.

God has also shown me favor and demonstrated love from an Agape perspective through my wife. She has stood by my side through my various personalities. I always strived to be her favorite person, and by default, I became her favorite husband. She has been a faithful partner, supporting me even when I embarked on new business ventures. She ensures that our businesses are done correctly, often going above and beyond my efforts. As a mother, she is exemplary. I have not witnessed a more dedicated and compassionate mother in my lifetime. She deeply loves her family and has grown into a great leader. She handles whatever challenges arise within our family, both internally and externally, always finding a way to forgive. She serves her community with gratitude, willingly embracing opportunities to help those less fortunate. She holds a bachelor's degree in education from the University of Arizona, fulfilling her family's value of higher education. Her appreciation for her parents and love for the elderly are her gifts. Yahweh looks favorably upon those who are willing to submit to their parents even when they are grown and can take care of themselves. She doesn't seek accolades or wealth; instead, she cherishes relationships with her family and friends. These attributes are what I deeply admire and find favor in my wife.

Likewise, my three children have found favor with their father. They are the joy of my life and a living testament to Yahweh's favor in my life. Despite the complexities surrounding Tomari's birth during the conception of the twins, my boys have remained healthy. They share a deep love for one another and diligently protect each other's honor and the honor of our family. Educationally, our family has excelled, with all five of us being honors students for most of our educational journeys. Additionally, we have all displayed exceptional athletic abilities. Coaching them during their high school years was one of my greatest accomplishments in life.

Coaching Basketball

I have always been actively involved in youth athletics, whether it was coaching or working in the administration. My incredibly supportive wife volunteered as the team mom, effectively running the program. The organizations we worked with respected the values we shared, particularly the importance of a healthy family structure to support the needs of the community. I coached high school and AAU teams, which comprised talented college-bound athletes. Together with a few parents, we sponsored the Arizona Dynasty basketball club and the Tucson Road Runners. I was a board member and coach. Our staff consisted of knowledgeable and teachable parents, and our primary goal was to provide opportunities for less fortunate athletes to showcase their talents on a larger platform. We played against formidable competition and remained highly competitive.

An interesting turn of events occurred when I had to coach my oldest son, Martio Jr.'s, high school basketball team in a summer league tournament. The high school coach decided to coach against his own team with his club team, and they convincingly defeated us. However, this experience ignited my interest in becoming a high school basketball coach. I decided to apply for the head coach position at Flowing Wells High School despite having no prior basketball coaching experience. Once again, God granted me favor, and I was given the opportunity. Coaching became one of the most memorable chapters of my life. The hard work and dedication exhibited by those young men were truly inspiring. Together, we instilled in them the belief that they were winners.

We experienced immediate success as a team. In my first year as coach, we reached the playoffs. My team consisted of exceptional students and athletes who had never been given hope or direction before. I spent each day practicing with them and providing encouragement. My captain, Jesus Campos, eventually became my best player and a true leader. Players like Jobe, Gabriel, Brandon, Richard, Josh, and our 15-man roster Riley all grew into better men. I successfully unified them, and our record for that year was 18 wins and 6 losses. We received various accolades, and the media and news articles named me coach of the year for our region. To top it all off, my son Martio Jr. was voted player of the year in our region, while Tomari and Demari were named to the All-Freshman team despite playing on the varsity team as freshmen. It was an incredible and challenging time in my life. I give my all to every endeavor I undertake, and coaching consumed me mentally. The level of competition demanded my utmost attention to detail. Making it to the playoffs wasn't enough; we aimed to reach the championship the following year. Yes, it consumed me, but it was all worth it.

Chapter 5

The Transition

During my third year of coaching, I had higher expectations, not just for myself; I was seeking accountability from the high school athletic world as a whole. Flowing Wells had become a well-known name in Arizona, and with the newfound attention, we were invited to participate in tournaments. We played in the Arizona State University summer tournament, where I had the privilege of spending time with Bobby Hurley. However, our team was ill-prepared for that level of competition. We were clearly outmatched throughout the entire weekend, losing by an average of 15 points per game. My seniors and juniors were all on vacation, so I was traveling with junior high school students who had recently made the team. They hadn't developed under their previous coach at the lower school levels, and they complained that my coaching style was too demanding. I expected a lot from everyone I coached, including myself. Excellence was the standard.

After a long summer, the basketball season began, and we faced some rough moments. We lost a couple of close games, and I was emotionally drained. It seemed like we couldn't recover from the heartbreak of those initial losses. Each game seemed to have a crucial call or no-call that changed the outcome. Evan Nelson Richer, the best friend of my twins, was particularly challenging to face. He played his freshman year at Mountain View High School before transferring to Salpointe High School. He eventually continued his basketball career at Harvard University. Yes, Harvard, not Howard (although I have a great appreciation for HBCUs). Personally, I didn't know any Harvard graduates, so I was immensely proud of him. However, during one game, he seemed to be allowed to take five steps, resulting in a game-winning bucket. I had a perfectly planned play to prevent him from even touching the ball, but sometimes things don't go as planned. I voiced my frustrations to the Athletic Director, hoping for some support or understanding, but instead, he became critical and showed no concern.

The following week, we played against Pushe Ridge High School in a close game with a great atmosphere. We led by three points with 14 seconds left on the shot clock. After a huddle, we needed to inbound the ball and advance it past half-court to secure the victory. However, nerves got the best of us, and Demari turned the ball over on the inbounds play. Fortunately, we played outstanding defense and regained possession. Demari, frustrated by his mistake, made it worse by slamming the ball into the ground with great force. I was expecting a technical foul to be called, but to my surprise, the referees showed favor toward us and did not make the call. I called a timeout to regroup for the final possession and asked Demari why he was willing to jeopardize the team. I explained the selfishness of his actions, driven by his frustration with himself. His response was not positive, and my reaction was equally negative. I headbutted him in the heat of the moment. It was an instinctive, regrettable action. He slid down the bench, and I immediately helped him up, feeling remorseful afterward. I reported the incident to my supervisor and even contemplated suspending myself. However, my Athletic Director convinced me that it wasn't warranted in this particular situation. For that, I found favor with him. Finally, progress was being made in our relationship. For the next week's game against Salpointe, something frustrating happened again. The twins' best friend, Major Deng (who went on to continue his college career at Pepperdine University), was allowed to goaltend several potential baskets before halftime. Feeling frustrated and seeking an explanation, I approached the referees during halftime, but they completely ignored me. I even told them I would do whatever it took to get their attention, even if it meant getting thrown out of the game. Well, they didn't waste any time fulfilling that request. It was embarrassing to find myself, in my third year of coaching, behaving like a rookie.

    I requested another meeting with my Athletic Director, hoping for a better outcome. Unfortunately, things didn't go well this time. We exchanged heated words, and he accused me of always playing the victim. I took offense to his comment and told him that his remarks were disrespectful and racist. We constantly disagreed on the fairness of the system, and it was clear that our goals were misaligned. Ultimately, we decided to part ways. This happened during the third week of the season, and I made the difficult decision to quit my team in the middle of the season. It was a devastating experience, but I felt there was no other healthy way to reconcile the relationship. I didn't feel appreciated or respected, and I felt like I was slowly losing myself.

    The ongoing conflicts and disagreements had taken a toll on both sides. As a result, I transferred my boys to Gregory School, a

Chapter 5

college preparatory school with a strong basketball program. They offered us free tuition through a scholarship. The twins' basketball careers flourished at Gregory School, where they went on to win two state championships. Academically, they excelled and graduated with honors, standing among a group of students destined to become doctors, lawyers, and business owners. My boys graduated in the top 5% of their class. Favor always finds my family because we position ourselves for it.

Chapter 6

Chasing Purpose

> "your purpose is God's pleasure; your pleasure is God's purpose."

WITHOUT UNDERSTANDING THIS phrase, many Kingdom citizens may find themselves caught in a conundrum. Life may appear aimless, and the search for purpose can feel like a never-ending whirlwind of confusion. You strive to break free from this monotonous bubble. Circumstances can shape your perception, especially if you grew up poor in America without the privilege of great teachers in financial literacy. In such situations, you find yourself working tirelessly, and when you are not working, you are too tired to have any fantastic visions of the American dream. Your sacrifice of time for money means you never grasp the opportunity to capture a part of this dream and make it happen. It may seem like everyone is compromising their values to achieve success. But is that the only way? The Word of God prepares us for a reality filled with power, not an unrealistic dream.

However, if you're not careful with the Word of God and its practical application, life can become even more confusing. It's important not to twist the Word for personal gain. For example, you may desire abundant blessings in your life while remaining humble. Can you truly have both? Or you might aspire to exhibit strong, confident leadership without being perceived as a narcissist. The challenge lies in commanding attention without being overbearing. You want to serve your community wholeheartedly without neglecting your family. The answer is to involve your family in community service alongside you. Living in the presence of the Holy Spirit and being of earthly good to your fellow brothers and sisters go hand in hand. Your servitude is a reflection of your righteousness; there's no way around it.

Searching for purpose externally often leads to dead ends. When you shift your focus inward and seek revelation of your purpose, you'll find a sense of peace beyond comprehension. The King has already provided all the resources we need for our purpose; we simply need to align ourselves with His promises. We must embrace covenant living, starting with following the Ten Commandments, and pass down this wisdom to future generations so that we always know "Who we belong to."

By keeping His commandments, God will bless you openly before others. He delights in demonstrating His power and strength by allowing mankind to wield His extraordinary powers. We have been blessed with various gifts that can be likened to superpowers when we are led by the Spirit of God. Scripture continually reminds us of this truth.

3 John 1:2–4 states, "Beloved, I wish above all things that you may prosper in everyway and [that your body] may keep well, even as [I know] your soul keeps well and prospers. In fact, I greatly rejoiced when [some of] the brethren from time to time arrived and spoke [so highly] of the sincerity and fidelity of your life, as indeed you do live in truth [the whole Gospel presents]. I have no greater joy than this, to hear that my spiritual children are living their lives in the truth."

Did you know that God desires your life to be filled with indescribable joy (1 Peter 1:8)? He doesn't want us to wait until we're old and ready to depart this world to serve Him. Ecclesiastes 12:1 advises, "Remember now thy Creator in the days of thy youth, while the evil days come not, nor the years draw nigh, when thou shalt say, I have no pleasure in them." Keep in mind that you are not your own but God's property, His child. Approach Him while you are young and innocent, before the days of evil surround you from all sides, and while you are still free from worldly pleasures. Embrace Him while you have much life left to enjoy.

In Philippians 2:13–15, verse 13 states, "For you may be young but it's not in your own strength, for it is God who is at work within you (energizing and creating in you the power and desire) to will and to work for His good pleasure and satisfaction and delight." In verse 14, we are instructed not to grumble, find fault, or complain against God (for it is for His purpose that you live). Do not question or doubt yourselves, for Yahweh has made you capable of fulfilling His purpose. In verse 15, it tells us that in fulfilling that purpose, you will show yourselves blameless, innocent, and uncontaminated, children of the Most High God, without blemish (faultless, unrebukable) in the midst of a crooked and wicked generation (spiritually perverse), and you will shine like bright lights (stand out) in this dark world.

What is Philippians about? Who wrote it? Who is it written to? Philippians was the first of the churches that Apostle Paul founded. The Gospel of Jesus Christ was yet young. He received a vision to start this church in Acts 16:9– 40. It was the first major penetration of the Gospel among the Gentiles. Paul found little fault with this church; they learned young, so it stuck. He was encouraging the church to keep up this joy and continue to rejoice (which appears at least 16 times in this letter). This book reveals the joy of a faithful lifestyle, living for Yahweh's Kingdom.

Let's delve into Philippians 2. In verse 13, the author emphasizes that God works in us, empowering us to fulfill His good pleasure. He gives us the strength and ability to carry out what pleases Him. Paul advises the church in Philippi to do all things without murmuring but to abide in God's truth, fulfill His purpose, and exercise His power. Sometimes, in our youthfulness, we may feel like we have arrived and question the authority of our parents, teachers, leaders, and even God. However, God instructs us to obey our parents (Ephesians 6:1), and the Bible also tells us that there is no authority in place on earth that God didn't ordain (Romans 13:1). Regardless of what we encounter, we must remember that God is in control.

The power and authority given to us through the blood of the Lamb make us blameless and harmless. Proverbs teaches us that we are not defined by the company we keep. Under the guidance of the Holy Spirit, I would advise you to separate yourself from the crowd (2 Corinthians 6:17). The enemy tries to group us with the tare (unholy world) and attack us with our past sins. However, we have the Word of God to combat him. 2 Timothy 2:15 encourages us to study the Word and show ourselves approved. When we know the Word and understand that God declares us not guilty, the opinions and blame of others hold no weight. If God is for us, who can be against us? Satan only attacks the innocent. Every time we repent, we are considered innocent in the eyes of God. Our innocence is our power. We are not burdened by confusion or guilt. We can connect with the Father and have the power to resist sin and the authority to tread upon serpents, just like our Lord and Savior, Jesus Christ.

As children of Yahweh, our power in this world is not based on our physical stature or intellectual abilities. Our power is assessed based on our obedience and the truth that we are children of Yahweh. Despite our shortcomings, we still have victory through Christ Jesus. The truth upsets the enemy of the Kingdom of Yahweh, who continually seeks to cause God's children to fail. He wants to be the father and leader. However, he cannot change the fact that our true Father is God. This revelation carries great authority. Once we grasp the principles of the Kingdom and accept our adoption, no one can take away our sonship. Our Father God has given us an inheritance of His Kingdom here on earth, just as it is in heaven. This Kingdom empowers us to have dominion over all aspects of life and grants us creative and healing abilities. We are meant to have authority in every area of life, except when it comes to dominating one another.

He gives us these truths to counteract the evils of this world. They serve as a counterculture to the distorted perception of truth that we have been conditioned to accept. It's like a microscope that brings clarity to the distorted views of righteousness embedded in our society. It splashes purity onto us in this perverted world.

In this generation, we encounter various forms of perversion, such as stealing, killing, destruction, drug and alcohol abuse, homosexuality, adultery, and more. However, Yahweh can and will deliver us from the consequences of these actions. It requires taking responsibility (repentance) and making a change. This determines whether we will accept Him into our hearts. You may ask, "Why do I keep failing repeatedly and ending up in the same place?" Look within yourself first. I dare to suggest that a significant part of it is the lust of the flesh—the desire for something because it feels good. Another factor may be the lust of the eyes— the allure of things that appear good, leading us to do whatever it takes to obtain them. The last hindrance to a successful journey is the pride of life—thinking we deserve and should have it all. Philippians 4:6–8 advises us: "I say to you that you better check yourself before you wreck yourself."

When you feel like you are directionless and don't have any goals, you are not living with purpose. You are simply going through life aimlessly, without seeking to accomplish anything for the benefit of others or yourself. Your relationship with God is likely broken or disconnected, and it may even be nonexistent. This dysfunction affects your ability to have intimate relationships with others. Most of the intimate relationships in your life lack passion. It becomes a familiar process because we see our lives mirroring our parents and family history. The curse becomes ingrained, and we learn to live with it, considering it normal. But living with that kind of normalcy means we are truly lost. We have little control over our lifestyle, and we are constantly emotionally drained. We feel hurt by the very people we would sacrifice ourselves for. However, we need to realize that this hurt is selfish. It is their choice how they want to live their lives. The contradictions of life have always thrown you off balance because you allow the circumstances of the world to dictate your attitude. Your only hope was to believe deep in your heart that you would escape that life as soon as possible. Turn your triumphs into a transformative conflict.

When is enough money truly enough? Do you have time to fulfill your commitments? What do you want to be remembered for? After asking these questions, search within yourself and rediscover self-love. People are blessed with the ability to watch others perform on TV or similar platforms. However, in reality, they often fail to focus on what is happening around them and miss out on their own blessings.

What Is My Purpose?

I am a serial entrepreneur, so I am always seeking business opportunities to take me to the next level. As a youth, my passion was football, but after exhausting all possibilities for a prosperous career and facing disappointment, I took a regular corporate job at a rental center. Unfortunately, that didn't turn out well. My general manager falsely accused me of stealing, and it became clear that corporate America wasn't the path for me to succeed. My manager made a felonious allegation; granted, he was the only one available to move the item. After a back injury, I had to apply for a worker's compensation claim. The company did not believe me, and they investigated me for a year and offered severance pay for my resignation.

Following that, I became a concert promoter for ROI Entertainment and ROI Records, Inc. I booked some of the most renowned rap artists for my events. But even that wasn't fulfilling enough, so I ventured into the music industry as an artist. I joined my brother's rap group, L.A.D., which later became MadLad due to another artist using the same name. We experienced local success and gained regional recognition, but it became overwhelming. So, I made a transition away from the entertainment industry, which ultimately saved my family and my soul. This maturing process led me to become an ordained minister, preaching in the church. I have developed a deeper faith by living in the Kingdom Dominion.

In 1993, I attended Barber school to learn a trade. I realized I couldn't continue doing unproductive work for those who oppressed my people. I was on a mission. I completed school in a record time of 7 months without missing a day. I became more focused and started to take control of my destiny. I started regaining a vision for my purpose. I was cutting hair while also preaching.

During my second year at Al's Barbershop, my brother, cousin, friend, and partner, Laron, kept reminding me that Christ was calling me back. My anointing light was flickering, as I was more concerned about pleasing the world with my music than pleasing God. I didn't want to hear him or see his face every day. When he strolled behind his chair, I knew he was going to say the same thing. "God gone get you, boy. He's calling you. Come back home." I listened to him for about two months, over and over, saying, "God gone get you. Come home." Finally, one day, at the mention of the name of Jesus, I broke down in tears. It was a refreshing experience. I had not cried in years. It was the most amazing feeling that I had experienced in a long time. I did not know I could cry like that. I have been crying ever since when I talk about the goodness of Jesus.

Doors began to open for me after I fully accepted Christ as my Lord and Savior. I started my own barbershop business and had the opportunity to coach my children at my Alma Mater, Flowing Wells High School. Each year I was there, I was blessed to impart the Spirit of God, a winning attitude, and a successful season. I was voted coach of the year by the sports analysts and my peers. My children were all stellar student-athletes, they all graduated with an A average, and they also played at the pinnacle of athletics, receiving all the accolades possible for sports. My twins, Tomari and Demari,

Chapter 6

even won their team's two state championships. That season brought significant emotional and spiritual growth to my life, with its trials and triumphs.

I focused more on imparting and influencing my family's views rather than letting the world's views influence them. I was not perfect at all; in fact, I made some major mistakes. One such mistake was headbutting one of my sons during a team timeout, and I retired a few weeks after that incident. I realized that the spirit of competition drives me to a focus that may be destructive in some areas. I focus on my goals with intention. When I have a desire to move forward, I do not let anyone or anything get in the way of my focus. My beautiful wife is the only person who can cause me to lose focus. When I have a disagreement with her, it can throw off my balance, as our household functions best when in harmony, so I try to resolve it immediately. I have had various other adventures, or what some may call jobs, but I approach them all with the intention of glorifying God through my lifestyle and efforts. I am never not working because my brain never rests, and I don't sleep very much. When I am awake, I am continually praying and interceding for God's people, pressing forward to receive wisdom to lead them out of captivity. I have never made a lot of money, but most people perceive me as successful. I can't say that yet because my story isn't complete yet. One thing that I do believe is that I am one of the wealthiest people on earth in spirit and faith. I gained that confidence when I received Christ. By the grace of God, I have been a faithful, loving husband. I have raised my children and trained them in the Word of God. They carried the Gospel as boldly and confidently as their earthly father. My children know I am only a surrogate to get them to their real Father. I taught them that from the beginning.

If we continue living within the context of this chapter, we will discover that our purpose is already within us. I didn't seek a purpose; I followed Christ and the leading of the Holy Spirit, and my purpose is continually being revealed. Your purpose awaits your call.

Chapter 6

Flowing Wells head coach Martio Harris calls out to an official during the first quarter.

Chapter 7

Chasing Wholeness

WHO OR WHAT is shaping your thoughts, and what are you talking about? 1 Corinthians 14:37 says, "If anyone thinks and claims that he is a prophet [filled with and governed by the Holy Spirit of God and inspired to interpret the divine will and purpose in preaching or teaching] or has any other spiritual endowment, let him understand (recognize and acknowledge) that what I am writing to you is a command of the Lord. But if anyone does not recognize [that it is a command of the Lord], he is disregarded and not recognized by God."

In modern America and other countries around the world, we have been taught that the spiritual gifts that God has given us were only for the people of the biblical era. In case you didn't know, I am here to tell you that we are still in the biblical era. As we speak, the Holy Spirit still guides and inspires us to write chapters for the New Testament. The dispensation of Grace and the Kingdom reign are still ongoing. In 1 Corinthians 14, Brother Paul encourages the Corinthians not to let others influence them to neglect or disregard the gifts that God has given them. Sometimes, we allow the thoughts and opinions of others to influence our own. The mind is delicate; it can be deceived, influenced, and subtly convinced to conform to the status quo.

What has the storm of modernization done to your mind? Modernity often promotes a mindset that anything goes. Have your modernized thoughts led to prosperity or despair? Have they brought you to a state of selfsufficiency or dependence on God?

During our transition to this modernized mindset, there are three basic belief systems that we may have become accustomed to:

The relativist mindset says whatever you believe is okay. This mindset depends on what you feel, think, or what your situation is. This train of thought believes that there are no absolutes. They try to use the Scripture against itself. They use texts such as Hebrews 11:31

to say that Rehab lied, and it was counted to her as faith. Relativists believe that there is no such thing as truth. People in this group believe that as long as it helps you get through the day, it is alright for profit, and profiting themselves is their main goal. Ecclesiastes 12:13–14, John 12:48, and Romans 14:11–12 are all scriptures that dispel that fable. The danger in that train of thought is that there is no foundation, faith, or reward. This group does not have the notion of sharing because everything is about self-preservation. God will wink at this until they are introduced to the truth (Acts 17:30; James 1:26). Relativists believe that your beliefs should be kept to yourself (Jude 3, 4; Jude 23, 24). We know as disciples that quiet belief is useless belief (Matthew 16:5).

Another mindset or belief system is privatization. This mindset says it's your belief, so keep it to yourself. This belief system is so tentative that it is not strong enough to bind us together as a community. We lose our capacity to belong. It gives us no accountability for our behavior, which gives us little to no influence on the behaviors of others, so behavior eventually gets out of control.

The last belief system is pluralism. This is the system the U.S.A. embraces. This belief system says whatever you're into is alright as long as you believe in something outside of yourself. The U.S.A. frowns upon atheists (people who don't believe there is a God), but we are taught to be tolerant or embrace everybody else's beliefs. Pluralism is also referred to as "paganism." It teaches that different religions are true even though they contradict one another. Pluralism contradicts the biblical teaching that there is one absolute Supreme Being. Isaiah 43:10 declares, "'You are My witnesses,' says the Lord, 'and My servant whom I have chosen, that you may know and believe Me, and understand that I am He. Before Me there was no God formed, nor shall there be after Me.'" Isaiah 45:5 states, "I am the Lord, and there is no other; There is no God besides Me. I will gird you, though you have not known Me." Acts 4:12 states, "Nor is there salvation in any other, for there is no other name under heaven given among men by which we must be saved."

Personally, I have always remained steadfast in my doctrine, making it difficult to sway my beliefs. I am outspoken about my convictions, even in a world filled with various religious beliefs and doctrinal differences within the Christian faith, and I will go tell it on the mountains.

Chapter 7

Taking The Kingdom Home To Religion

In my work environment, I strive to maintain impartiality and non-judgment toward individuals' belief systems and personal values. I hold certain standards for creating a conducive environment for successful work practices. I also remain open to personal growth through the influential actions of others within that environment. While I respect different ways of thinking, I personally acknowledge and proclaim God as the Most High on a daily basis. I do not aim to offend anyone with my beliefs or opinions. It is important for me to share what I believe so that I can contribute to the manifestation of God's Kingdom on earth. I have discovered that even if I were not a believer, I would still find value in using the Bible as a practical guide for living, guiding me toward possibilities beyond my imagination.

The Fight To Bring Home The Word Of God

This may pose challenges in households that are bound by deep religious strongholds that did not prove effective for our ancestors. These strongholds have left us paralyzed by the opinions of fellow church members. We become overly concerned with avoiding disappointment and upsetting the organizational structure of the church, to the point where we only take action when someone else upsets us. Our religious beliefs have taken over our logic. However, we are encouraged to test the work of God and witness His faithfulness in providing and producing edifying results. Our commitment and confidence can waver when our partner in the relationship does not share or accept the teachings and doctrines that inspire us. I encountered a similar issue in my household during the early years of my marriage. My wife felt that I was going overboard by insisting on family Bible study sessions almost every night. My intention was to instill in my children the importance of always honoring God in everything they do. With time, I learned to strike a balance in my personal relationships. I came to understand that I was imposing my personal beliefs on others, and I have since become more adaptable and approachable in my presence.

Sadly, one of my spiritual sons attempted to introduce the Gospel of the Kingdom and alignment to his Catholicraised spouse.

Balance - The Greatest Chase Ever

He was on fire for the Lord and deeply desired to please everyone. He wanted to please God and impress his peers at the same time. The conflict between the flesh and the spirit intensifies whenever you decide to press into the Lord. He started to receive resistance at home when talking about his beliefs. The distance between his wife and him started to impact his actions, movements, and decisions. One day, while indulging in pornography online, he stumbled upon a video featuring a woman who looked identical to his wife in a bedroom that resembled theirs, engaging in a sexual act with a man. He said that was exactly how she performed. I was floored when he showed me the video and asked me to verify who it was. It was a deeply distressing revelation. After a conversation with his wife, he chose to believe her explanation of a mistaken identity. Although they reconciled temporarily, the relationship never fully recovered, and the Word of God was abandoned in their household. The relationship eventually ended in a messy divorce. His wife was very cunning during the process, and he never had any legal counsel during the dissolution process. She ended up with full custody of their two children and was also awarded child support. She had a much higher income than he did, but she was still awarded support. The divorce caused him to have a nervous breakdown. He could no longer control his emotions. He frequently engaged in heated arguments and near-physical altercations with students on a daily basis. He would come to work with an aggressive attitude toward everyone. Sometimes, he would come into the office, pull out a razor, and shave his head rigorously while daring someone to say something. I understood the depth of his heartache, so I tolerated the blatant disregard and disrespect in the environment I allowed him to express himself in. He began proclaiming that God was not real and exploring different religions and sexual practices. All the activities with different spiritual sources and different beliefs overwhelmed his ability to function effectively in a professional environment. Eventually, he did me a favor by not showing up for work when I was out of town, claiming that his new girlfriend was preventing him from leaving. Fed up with his excuses, I made the decision to close down my night classes, signaling that his services were no longer required by our organization. Although I continue to pray for him, I am aware that the enemy will continue to torment his soul until he finds firm conviction in his beliefs.

Chapter 7

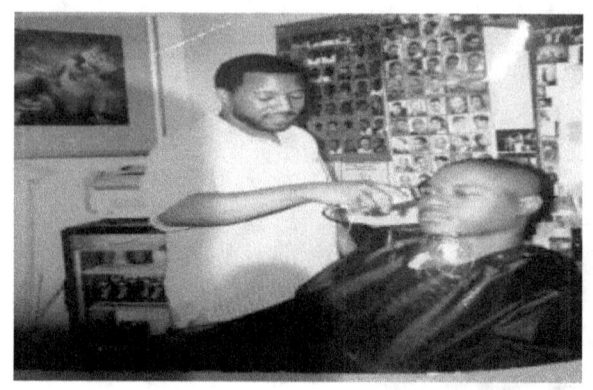

Chapter 8

Self-Contained Underwater Breathing Apparatus

ARE YOU SELFISH or selfless? Upon whom do you rely for your needs? God has bestowed upon us a breathing apparatus for the earth called the Holy Spirit. Prior to creating us, God provided the world with all that it would require to sustain us. He gave us elements such as oxygen, hydrogen, carbon dioxide, and more, intended to maintain balance within our bodies. He had a concept: "I will make man like Me to redeem the earth" (Genesis 1:26). Reflect on that. This amazing God we serve thought so highly of the earth that He would redeem and replenish it through man (Genesis 1:22). Most of us may have never fully grasped the truth that the first commandment given to man was to redeem the earth and restore it to a glorious Kingdom where the presence of the Living God reigns. It is an awe-inspiring task that God did not take lightly. Therefore, He did not merely create man; He made man in His own image (to resemble Him). Not only that, He made man in His likeness (with His character and nature). To ensure that man could never remain defeated, even in failure, God bestowed upon us His power to dominate every life form, except for one another. God was filled with excitement over this magnificent being He created. He loves and cherishes mankind, for man is God's pride and joy.

With these preceding declarations in mind, we should understand that God has a purpose for every individual ordained to live on this earth by Yahweh (2 Timothy 1:9). The primary purpose is to bring glory to God by reestablishing His Kingdom wherever we go (Mark 16:15). God did not leave us to fend for ourselves; rather, He provided us with an oxygen tank, just as we would need for underwater scuba diving.

Let us break it down and compare the processes. John 5:30 states, "I can of mine own self do nothing." Do you realize that everything you do outside of God ultimately amounts to nothing? John 17:5

says, "Glorify thou me with thine own self." Philemon 19 states, "You owe me even your own self." God wants to know who you truly are. He wants you to recognize your worth. In John 15:4, He declares that if He is in you and you are in Him, you will produce great things. However, without Him, you can do nothing. Understanding these truths should prevent you from being judgmental towards others who may not have committed to the same level as you have. Brother Paul writes to the Corinthian church in 1 Corinthians 4:3, "I cannot even judge myself because I do not know what I am going to do next." These scriptures serve as evidence that we should not undertake anything independent of God if we expect to witness supernatural results.

Once we fall into the fallacy of self-improvement, we must exercise restraint or be confined. We need the right temperament to handle life's challenges. We cannot discard our oxygen tank because we may encounter a shark. We require that tank to effectively combat it. Remember, the tank (the Holy Spirit) contains the resources we need to secure a victorious outcome. In 1 Corinthians 7:7–9, Paul states, "I wish that all men were like myself in this matter of self-control." God has ways of boxing us in when we venture into territories He has not yet granted us. He may bestow them upon us in due season (Ecclesiastes 3:1).

While God is working on your transformation, He desires for you to remain under His providence. He does not want you to venture into the devil's domain and then call upon Him when you are in trouble. Rather, He wants you to seek Him before embarking on any adventures. He desires for you to become a new creature under His authority (2 Corinthians 5:17). According to Colossians 1:22–23, if you continue to be grounded in your faith, He will make you holy, blameless, and beyond reproach in His sight. It requires great faith to submit to someone's authority (Matthew 8:9). We must learn to keep our own bodies under subjection, which enables us to submit to authority (1 Corinthians 9:27). God has everything under His subjection, yet He still does not force anyone to obey Him. He desires to subject all things to redemption, even though our perspective may not align with His (Hebrews 2:8). Each person will be subject to something. Have you decided to whom or what you are subject, or, in other words, do you know what you are under the influence and authority of? God or evil?

So, what should we do with this breath of life? Is it like a fleeting puff of smoke to you? Or is it a refreshing wind that is necessary to fulfill your purpose? Is it divine inspiration or merely an angry and vital breath? Is it used sensibly, or is it employed to destroy and tear others down (Job 17:1)? Acts 17:24–25 tells us that God gives us life, breath, and all things.

God has given us these things (our lives) to be used for His purpose. We are instruments that should not be wasted. Each of us has a specific purpose. We are fearfully and wonderfully made (Psalms 139:14). We are peculiar (beyond the usual, special to God) (Titus 2:14; 1 Peter 2:9). Have you discovered the purpose that God has for you?

These are some key points that I believe God wants you to take from this study:
1. Kingdom people have the will and right to overcome all sin through the power of God.
2. Kingdom people remain under the anointing and glory of God.
3. Kingdom people rejoice in the breath of life.
4. Kingdom people are created for a specific purpose.

Trekking Your Own Path.

I have an example of someone who possesses a high set of values based on universal truths of kindness, servitude, responsibility, and a sincere sense of common decency. Interestingly, I have yet to witness him ascribe to any particular religion. However, whenever I am in his presence, I feel a spirit of love that can only come from Yahweh. This person is my cousin, Lamonte Hunley, who was chosen by Yahweh and my mother to provide me with shelter, protect my access to the world, and help me become a responsible citizen. I moved in with him and his brother, Ricky Hunley, who is a college hall of famer and my big cousin. I am proud to say that between my junior and senior years of high school, my life changed dramatically.

It all began when my family was stationed in Darmstadt, Germany. While I usually had a good sense for choosing friends, the crowd I associated with there was rowdy and caused a lot of trouble. I found myself involved in a "gang fight" in the middle of a hallway, which ultimately led to my expulsion in the second semester of my junior year. Yes, my 11th-grade year of high school went downhill. Faced with the consequences, my parents had a choice: either send me back to America or risk losing their military ranking, pay, and position. They made the wise decision, and off I went to Arizona. The flight was a seventeen-hour journey, and I arrived in Arizona with only a suitcase, some money I had saved, and a million dollars' worth of hope. I managed to earn a decent amount of money by bagging groceries at the Post Exchange Market (P.X.), and I even gave my mother a few thousand dollars to help with her bills. Boarding the Military Airbus flight, I embarked on a new chapter in the scorching desert heat of Arizona.

Welcome To Arizona

Quinton, my favorite cousin, picked me up from Tucson airport. It was freezing and snowing when I departed from Frankfurt Airport in Germany, but the weather in Arizona was quite different. As I stepped off the runway and took my first breath of desert air, I was taken aback. The dry heat was suffocating, and I almost hyperventilated.

Living and learning with my famous cousins as a young student-athlete felt like a dream come true. What made it even better was that they were hardly ever home because they were in the NFL. Ricky was playing for the Raiders at the time, and Lamonte was with the Colts. Lamonte's younger brothers and his close friends, Julius Holt and Ahee, were occasional visitors. Their house was a bachelor's paradise, equipped with all the luxuries and amenities one could imagine. It was an extravagant and picturesque 6,000square-foot mansion nestled in the foothills of the Tucson Estate mountains. The household included Ricky Hunley, the owner of the house, who stayed there when he wasn't with his wife, Camille. They actually met while he lived in that home, and they have been happily married for over 30 years, which shows his loyalty and perseverance to his mentees, like myself. Lamonte Hunley, my legal guardian, was the disciplinarian in the house. He upheld integrity, lawfulness, and order. He also coached my high school football team at Flowing Wells. Lamonte and Julius served as assistant coaches to John Kashner, the head football coach. When Lamonte wasn't with his

Chapter 8

beautiful and supportive wife of 29 years, Stephanie, he dedicated himself to empowering the young men on the team, including myself. Quinton, my partner in crime (may he rest in peace), was always involved in some kind of mischief with multiple women. Derek, the enforcer, was known for getting into fights. Kevin, the chameleon, had a knack for wrecking cars, fixing problems, and staying low-key. Julius Holt, also known as Q_Dog, was quite the ladies' man until he met his beautiful wife, Lisa, who eventually tamed him. Al, my friend who dealt drugs, had a kind heart. And lastly, Kenny Thomas, the patriarch of the family, served as the father figure. Everyone in the household lived together harmoniously and contributed their part. We did have a couple of incidents where the Jacuzzi flooded the house due to neglecting the water level, but aside from that, life was great.

My cousins were given a once-in-a-lifetime opportunity due to their academic and athletic achievements. Their exceptional gifts and talents allowed them to escape from an environment that was always hostile and offered limited chances for success. Rather than carrying a depressed attitude with them, they embraced the challenge of growing in this new environment. Our family learned to navigate this foreign territory with grace and honor, seizing the great opportunities it presented. As they understood the importance of policies and procedures, they were able to leverage their knowledge and secure influential positions. They demanded and earned authority while adhering to the necessary rules. They taught me the ways of a Classic Man, and I have embraced that training, carrying it in my mental and character Rolodex to this day. Charisma certainly wasn't lacking in their family, and they introduced me to a whole new world. When faced with this new environment, they operated with a sense of class and taught me to do the same.

Among them, Lamonte had the greatest impact on me because of his Christlike character. Although not religious in nature, he carried a righteous purity in his intentions. He utilized his influence and power to positively impact as many people as possible. His posture and demeanor were consistent with his character, and his words aligned with his actions. If he ever asked someone to do something for him, he would overcompensate them for their services. He firmly believes in the practice of giving and understands that you cannot outgive the King. I hold Lamonte, Ricky, and the other brothers in the highest respect and admiration. If I had to choose an earthly father, they would be at the front of the line. Congratulations, Kendra and Devin; your dad is a remarkable individual who leaves a lasting impression. Congratulations, Alexis and Kenady; your dad is truly amazing. These two qualities— legacy and leadership—are what they build. They serve as exceptional role models for young men and have exemplified the Self-Contained Underwater Breathing Apparatus, preparing their children for great success. They taught me the importance of accountability and independence.

Vacations were always an exciting yet nerve-racking time for my family. Personally, I am a minimalist and prefer to travel with as little luggage as possible. I can manage a week-long trip with just a book bag. On the other hand, my beautiful wife tends to pack enough for everyone. Growing up, we didn't have much money, so I truly value the financial stability we have now. Despite living off a barber's salary, we still enjoyed a great lifestyle. My wife and I made a decision early in our marriage to be available at all times to raise our children. She, being a college graduate, chose to become a homemaker for the sake of our children, while I generated sufficient income through my barbershops and other ventures. We have created countless wonderful memories together. Every year, we embark on a major family vacation. We have been to Kauai in Hawaii twice, as well as beautiful Costa Rica on two occasions. We have explored various destinations across Mexico, and our love for its beaches led us to purchase a retirement home there. We have also visited The Bahamas twice. I have lived in Germany. I don't want to visit there again. Actually, I don't know if I can. I was deported following a high school riot in which I was involved, leading to my expulsion. Currently, I am in the process of planning a trip to Africa as I develop a barbers app with developers located in Kenya.

Despite the fantastic destinations we have visited, our family vacations have often been marred by disappointing moments and disagreements. These incidents have always necessitated a mood adjustment. I am naturally high-strung, even when it comes to vacationing. I meticulously plan everything, and I have a small budget for unexpected expenses. I emphasize the importance of

Chapter 8

family togetherness, while others argue that vacation amenities should not be neglected. I've been labeled a cheapskate.

My children have only known living in the biggest house on the block throughout their lives. They don't require the luxury suites at Marriott; they simply want to be together and have fun. This topic has sparked heated discussions within our household due to the differing opinions among the five of us. Nonetheless, we have enjoyed many incredible experiences and captured lasting memories and photos from all around the world.

These vacations and family moments have served as inspiration for my Self-Contained Underwater Breathing Apparatus. I am grateful for the opportunity to lead and raise a faithful, God-fearing household. This unity is crucial in keeping us connected, engaged, and prepared for our mission.

Chapter 9

Balance

> "A false balance is an abomination to the LORD, but a just weight is his delight."
> – Proverbs 11:1

LIVING IN THE flesh presents its own set of challenges. Throughout life, we experience ups and downs and must strive to find balance to truly enjoy it. Balance lends way to keeping a certain amount of simplicity in life. When our lives are full of complications, it takes the wind out of our sails. We tend to just go with the flow. Sometimes we get overzealous when it comes to achievements and goals. We tend to get way out in the middle of the ocean on the huge, really fast waves. The ship's momentum seems to be full steam ahead. Once we get worn down, we begin to drift aimlessly with no direction.

Has this ever happened to you? Have you ever had a perfect plan to accomplish a goal? Most people tend to get started with great enthusiasm, but in the midst of the storm, they realize that the plan was a bit off and they don't have the stamina to complete the task. The participants did not count the cost. They did not know the wear and tear it would cause their bodies, minds, and relationships. I have been there. Being there taught me to work diligently to see the result before I begin. That is called an exit plan or vision. We must be visionaries to defeat our enemies successfully. They will attack your physical health, your spiritual health, and your emotional health. Stay grounded for the next challenge.

When the enemy tries to attack your physical health, remember 1 Corinthians 6:19–20: "Do you know that your body is the temple (the very sanctuary) of the Holy Spirit who lives in you, whom you have received (as a gift) from God? You are not your own." If someone gives you something valuable, you handle it with care. How do you respond when life's trials come crashing in? Do you still cherish and honor that gift? Do you take the best possible care of it? Or do you treat it as worthless, throwing it on the ground, dragging it through the mud, and spitting on it? If your response aligns with cherishing and caring for the gift, then you understand what God expects of you regarding your body (His dwelling place). If you resonate with the latter, then it's evident that you need a renewal of your mind.

God didn't expect you to be aligned with His will without paying a great price. In verse 20 of the same chapter, it says that you were bought with a price (purchased with preciousness, paid for, and made His own). If this resonates with you, then honor God and bring glory to Him with your body and soul. God desires you to be a faithful servant of His will. He has given you a domain to exercise authority over, but first, you must submit and subject yourself to His Heavenly Kingdom.

The Greek definition of the word "body" originates from "so de zo," which means to deliver, protect, heal, preserve, or save oneself, to do well, to be, make, or slave. Preserving your body for the glory of God means making it a safe dwelling place for Him— the cleanest place you can find. The goal is to invite the Spirit of the Living God to dwell within you. After receiving His guidance, you can deliver His message to the world as a powerful messenger and deliverer, bringing people from the Kingdom of Hell into the Kingdom of God. Yahweh expects us to be servants bound to His purpose. He will keep your body healthy. He will keep His light within you so that darkness and sickness cannot reside (for darkness and light cannot coexist). Yahweh covers you with the blood of His Son. Along with physical exercise to keep your body fit and healthy, watch what you eat and ensure you get adequate rest.

A temple in Greek is called "naos," which refers to a shrine, dwelling, sacred place, or central sanctuary. How do you view the temple that God has given you? Do you care for it as the central sanctuary of the Living God? Do you fill it with unhealthy products? What are you storing within it? If you were to analyze your body, what would it reveal about how well you have cared for it thus far? The mind of God should be at the center of your temple, which is your heart. Your heart serves as His sanctuary.

The Holy Spirit, known as "hagios" in Greek, denotes being sacred, pure, blameless, religiously consecrated, and a holy saint

Chapter 9

(one entity). What do you do for spiritual exercise? Do you read daily? Do you meditate (Psalms 1:2)? The only way to exercise your spirit is through the Word of God. Relying solely on external sources won't help you out. The Bible serves as your personal trainer. You don't even need to leave your home to receive a thorough workout. Just find a secluded place and request a meeting with your trainer. The more focused you are during this exercise, the more spiritually fit you will become. This trainer doesn't provide artificial substances like steroids for rapid growth; this exercise fosters pure growth. You won't face blame from others for cheating your way to the desired results. Your mind becomes aligned with Christ's as He takes His rightful place as the head of your life.

The spirit that God breathes into you is called "pneuma." It represents a current, breath, blast, or breeze. It encompasses the rational soul and holds your vital principles. A fresh breath from Yahweh imparts a distinctive disposition. It causes you to radiate, making you transcend human capabilities. It is the voice of angels and the life-giving spirit of your mind. To breathe in the right air, the atmosphere must be conducive to a spiritual breakthrough, not just a physical presence. The conditions must be set for the manifestation of Yahweh's power. You must exercise your mind in the proper environment to achieve optimal results. The air cannot be contaminated or polluted. The rational soul must be brought under submission and prepared to receive a divine breeze from God. The supplication will overthrow anything in your life that is not aligned with Him.

Ask yourself, "Am I getting the proper exercise for my mind, body, and spirit?"

Despite my efforts to simplify my life, I always had a lot going on. Whether it was purchasing property, preaching, or coaching children, I tended to stretch myself thin. I aged quickly because I couldn't handle the load, and without purpose and direction, I could not perform well. My wife, Telisha, is the person closest to me. She had to cope with the emotions that come with having a husband who takes on countless projects at once. The Bible tells us to serve the church but not to neglect our own households. I managed my commitments as if I were a juggler handling five balls and even a weight. If a heavier weight were thrown at me, I would adjust my technique and drop one or two of the other balls to be effective. I would pivot and give attention to the most important concern. Assessing the level of risk associated with each factor determines which ball is more valuable at any given time.

Balance is both a science and an art form. Paul said it is better to marry than to burn, but cohabitation can be one of the most challenging experiences when it comes to living a balanced lifestyle. The complexity arises from growing up in separate environments and then trying to harmonize your thoughts, beliefs, and ideologies to live together harmoniously. It can sometimes feel like you are constantly compromising. At other times, it feels like you are being trained for the betterment of the Kingdom. The Kingdom trains you to evaluate the good life and envision a prosperous family. Yet, at times, it may feel like your spirit and soul are being compromised. Growing up with my wife was like transitioning from an A-model relationship to an H-model relationship.

H-model Relationship

In an H-model relationship, each person is secure in their own personal goals. They walk together equally yoked, without relying on each other for strength or support.

When entering into intimate relationships, you fall in love and desire to be with that person every second of your life. You form a bond that should never be broken; it evolves into a covenant. If you are serious about the vow between you, the other person, and Yahweh, you should be in alignment, and the covenant will endure. This covenant requires a yoke or a shared understanding and agreement. The yoke represents a common position or stance that keeps your family united and focused on the goal. It helps fulfill the legacy of your family and provides a clear direction for the journey. Living with fewer distractions offers a better chance of getting the results that you would like to see. If you have that yoke together and do not let your worldly responsibilities and circumstances separate your relationships, Yahweh's way will withstand any attempts by the enemy to destroy your destiny. You will always come out standing strong.

Chapter 9

A-model Relationship

An A-model relationship is one where the husband and wife depend on each other for everything. If one person is absent, the other struggles to cope with life. There is an addictive personality and a significant amount of insecurity on someone's part. The more dependent we are on God, the less we rely on our own understanding. We get the leading of the Holy Spirit's power and authority and adhere to the Word of God when we are mature in faith. It will strengthen the yolk, and we will develop into two strong individuals. The parties are now interdependent and not codependent on one another. The parties are no longer leaning, but they are standing firm. They are still connected at their core. In relationships, the more you are able to obtain this type of situation, the healthier your relationships will be.

I have learned to embrace these principles in my everyday life, whether personal or business-related. I stand firm, allowing my partners and counterparts to stand on their own. I am there to support them when needed, but I also give them space to grow, fall, and regain confidence. I reassure them that they can succeed independently.

Balance is knowing the distinction between what you need and what you want. While it's important to attain many things you desire, it's equally crucial to have what you truly need. Furthermore, we should strive to balance our emotions, as it brings us closer to fulfilling our purpose and helps us overcome half of the challenges we face. By managing our commitments to community service and our responsibilities within our households, we can find satisfaction in both aspects. We must pay close attention to the details because spirituality cannot be separated from our daily walk. One will reveal and impact the other. I encourage you to seek greater balance on the spiritual side. When the enemy approaches, you will already be equipped with the guidance and tools to resist their snares and evil schemes. Safeguard your mind, heart, and spirit through reading the Word, meditation, and spending private time with Yahweh in prayer. He will continue to provide balance for your journey.

Stay Balanced; Keep Your Cool

    The unexpected event occurred on the day before I received my appointment as Youth Pastor at Agape Christian Community Church. Eventually, I obtained my Ordained Minister's license from there. It was a relatively calm day when I started receiving prank phone calls, with someone whispering threats of having a gun pointed at my head. In response, I instructed my coworkers and customers to leave through the back entrance. I stood there and confronted the situation head-on, challenging the caller. The call ended abruptly, and we resumed our work. It seemed that someone had attempted to scare me. My family was thriving, my business was flourishing, my ministry was advancing, and I felt a sense of buoyancy. A customer, whom I recognized as an associate of one of my brothers (Plado), entered my establishment and began acting nervously. He came very close to my face and demanded that I punch him. Initially, I took it as a joke, but he was serious. He did not laugh at all; he wanted "smoke" for real. He cocked back and then struck me forcefully under my right eye.

    I did not even get a chance to stop the shave that I was performing. At that point in my spiritual journey, my anointing was overwhelming and overflowing, and I didn't even feel the impact of the blow. He hit me as hard as he could, but it did not even feel like a mosquito bite. I remained in awe but knew I didn't want to harm him. I quickly considered the potential news headline: "Pastor Murders Young Man at Local Barbershop." I shook off the thought and chose not to retaliate. My armor bearer and best friend, Damien Little, who was cutting his clients next to me, swiftly restrained the young man in a headlock and took him outside. Our customers were ready to defend me as well. I understood the consequences and recognized that the enemy would use anything and anyone to deter me from my mission. He comes only to kill, steal, and destroy the hopes and dreams of Yahweh's faithful. I wasn't about to jeopardize my destiny. Instead, I attempted to calm the spirit and cast it out of him. While praying, he swung at me once again. This time, I maneuvered around the punch and applied a sleeper hold to subdue him. This wrestling move stifled his aggression, rendering him unconscious. When he eventually regained consciousness, he continued to threaten that he would return with his friends to kill me. I knew that Yahweh had me covered, so I dismissed his threats and carried on with my day as usual. The Bible teaches us not to touch or speak against Yahweh's anointed. Tragically, within a week, the young man met his demise. He was fatally struck by a rock at the gated guard entrance of Davis-Monthan Air Force Base. I wish the outcome could have been different. He had attempted to destabilize me, but he failed. It cost him his life. However, it propelled me to obtain my license and ordination within a year of that encounter.

I strive to juggle life like a master juggler, capable of managing a multitude of issues as long as they carry the same weight. However, when an emergency or unforeseen problem arises, I recognize the need to adjust my attention to detail. When confronted with something of a different weight, mass, or size, it's important to address it immediately with greater focus. Rather than dropping all the balls in failure, set one issue aside at a time. Use wisdom to prioritize your life and strive to please Yahweh first. When you're ready to press forward, Yahweh will handle the difficult work, and everything will fall into place. Avoid complaining when you complicate your life by taking on more than you can handle. Instead, shift your focus and realign yourself. The Bible warns that false measures or imbalances are abominations to the Lord, and no one wants to be an abomination. So live a balanced, healthy lifestyle of faith.

Are you prepared for the inevitable storms of life? What is your temperament when someone tries to provoke a reactive and unstable response from you? What mechanisms do you practice to ensure the appropriate response to tragedy? Are there any activities you can cut out to improve your balance?

Chapter 10

Chasing Acceptance

WHEN YOU FEEL like you lack direction and struggle to maintain focus long enough to accomplish your goals, it can be a sign that you are not living in alignment with your purpose. You may find yourself simply going through the motions of life, waiting for things to improve without actively working toward change. We have a lot to do, but nothing is ever completed. You engage in activities without any intention of completion; you just need something to occupy your time. However, these distractions, which could have been planned better, prevent you from being truly effective with your time. This lack of purpose and direction can also have a negative effect on your relationships, causing frugality and distance to creep in, leading to broken relationships.

Most of the time, when your family relationships are unstable and broken, it often reflects a broken relationship with God as well. Operating outside of wholeness hinders your ability to have intimate relationships with others, especially when both or all parties are broken. This distorted way of living prevents intentional living and perpetuates dysfunctional relationships as the norm, and we need others to control our emotional wellness. Being normal literally means that you are a conformist. You may appear to be flourishing and fitting in well on the surface, but the reality is that in moments of solitude, feelings of depression and emotional exhaustion may consume you. Joy becomes elusive, and you forget how to experience it.

Effects Of Trying To Be Accepted

When you find yourself trying to conform to your surroundings and maintain a facade to fit in, it can lead to a sense of self-righteous indignation. You may feel like your feelings have been hurt so much by the people you believed you would sacrifice your dying breath for if required. But they are so busy trying to live their journeys that they do not even recognize your feelings. You start to feel that hurt is selfish because it is still a choice. Are you self-righteous, or are you hurt? It does not matter which feeling describes your infliction. Everyone has their opinions. We have a decision to make about how we want to live our lives. The complexity of life's relationships will always cause you to feel off balance. We have to believe in what we believe in. If that is the stance you decided on, then move in that direction of teaching your faith. You have to always believe in your heart that you will always win. Make a plan to escape from unhealthy, destructive environments. Any environment that doesn't agree with your spirit, as soon as you can flee, get moving. Do not allow procrastination to hinder your personal growth anymore. Without a firm commitment to your faith, all significant decisions become a conflict. When is enough money enough? Do you have time to do what you have committed to do for others? Are you taking enough time for yourself? What do you want to be remembered for?

Find Yourself

Fall in love with yourself again. If you are not in love with the God-given grace and mercies bestowed upon us in this land, you are truly missing out on a tremendous blessing. Don't be plagued with inequality, iniquity, and the average "stinking thinking" human because you will not be able to experience the advantages of living with the benefit of the doubt that God is up to something good concerning you. The highest emotional peak that will be reached when watching other people who are blessed is an objective high. There's no real joy when you look at the wrong sources. The entertainment and information they can watch on their favorite TV shows form a spiritual space for demonic portals. We must limit the amount of influence from outside sources. Focus on what's really going on around you. Devise a plan that you can consistently and effectively complete by using your talents and gifts to generate some "now-faith" manifestation in that environment. The highest emotional peaks after self-reflection become your triumphs and victories. You become your own hero, your own biggest cheerleader, and your own best friend. Find a subjective upliftment when Yahweh blesses your visions.

You can't beat the impossible odds set up by society if you don't have a strategy. Don't rely on luck anymore. These are all generational dispositions and curses that are transferred through faulty training. Institutions, such as educational systems, churches, the workforce, and welfare systems, have perpetuated these curses, rendering their constituents subservient. It's important to recognize that many institutions in place today were built on lies, murder, and destruction. Without genuine repentance from the perpetrators, the cycle continues. The results of this lack of repentance bring curses upon future generations until true repentance occurs. Failure to break free from generational curses can destroy the fabric of a family. I personally struggled with this in the early years of my marriage. However, I made a decision not to perpetuate a broken family legacy and committed to breaking the curse.

The circumstances of my marriage were rapid and unexpected. We tied the knot exactly one year after meeting each other. Everybody speculated that we were hiding a pregnancy, but the truth was we were deeply in love and ready to commit to a lifetime together. She was my ride-ordie lady from day one.

My wife's family had worked hard to secure an uppermiddle-class lifestyle. They were well educated, and they ensured that their daughter was well educated and properly trained for success. On the other hand, I was a young black country boy with limited guidance or authority, coming from a broken family background. I was rough around the edges but ambitious, a diamond in the rough waiting to be discovered and polished. I decided to embark on a spiritual journey with God, believing that He was the only person I had to please. Being accepted was no longer going to hold me back.

The Meeting

I saw her from across the field at a social gathering called Juneteenth. I remember it like it was yesterday. I was there with my girlfriend and some friends, while the sexiest woman in the park was with her boyfriend and their companions. Despite the situation, I felt an undeniable attraction, and a voice inside me said, "That's your wife right there." I knew I had to make my move and claim what was mine. I devised a master plan to approach her. When she got into a fight with her boyfriend, I stepped in and got her number. She was intrigued by my assertiveness. She initially tried to play hard-to-get by ignoring my phone calls. At the time, I was a walk-on football player at the University of Arizona and also served as the scout team's hitting dummy for Desert Storm. After persisting for about a month, I sent her a message stating, "This is the last time I am calling you." If you pull that out and don't receive the right response, you have no chance. It was a make-or-break moment, and I wondered if my confidence overwhelmed her. From that point on, our love story unfolded over the course of 29 years and counting. However, our relationship didn't receive immediate approval from her parents, particularly her mother.

She Finally Called Me Back

The guy she was with didn't take the situation well and decided to confront me in front of his girlfriend. He tried to act tough and puffed out his chest a little too far, but my friends were happy to deflate it for him and give him what he was asking for. In the midst of the commotion, one of my friends accidentally hit my wife, who was trying to intervene and help her boyfriend. I quickly stepped in to stop the fight. Interestingly, earlier in the night, she had actually approached me, mistaking me for someone she knew. It was a chaotic evening, but I still managed to get her phone number. I knew she would be a challenge because she didn't return my calls for months. I had already called my mom and told her that I had met the woman that I was going to marry. I was convinced she was the one I wanted to marry, so I made one final call while I was in my hotel room at training camp. My message was straightforward: "This will be the last time I call you if you don't call me back." Within an hour, she finally called me back. That interaction set the tone for our relationship. I had to be firm to get her attention. We faced challenges with other men, including her exboyfriends, who eventually realized they had no chance. I had found the person worth changing for and being accepted by. After four months of pursuing her, she finally agreed to a special first-date dinner. I chose a restaurant, Denny's. Yes, Denny's.

At the time, that was my idea of a romantic night out. I had a lot to learn in that department, and my wife still reminds me of that. I impressed her enough to add a movie to our dinner, and I knew I was making progress. We ended up watching Basic Instinct, which got us both worked up. They must have put a spirit on that scene where Sharon Stone had her legs crossed because, after the movie, we found ourselves at my wife's apartment, ready to take things further. Before we could make the room foggy, we were interrupted by a phone call. It was her friend, Crystal. She had attempted suicide. We rushed to the hospital, and fortunately, Crystal recovered. In that moment, we saw each other's reactions to intense situations and appreciated one another's support through good times and bad. From that point on, we fully accepted each other and have been experiencing life together ever since.

Meeting The Parents

When the time came to meet my wife's parents, which was about four months after we first met and a month after our first date, I was filled with excitement and a bit of awe. Her family was a successful, middle-class black family with both the biological mother and father still together in the household—something I aspired to have. I knew deep down that I had to marry this queen. Not only did she have the right appearance, but she also carried herself with grace in public, something I knew would be important as I pursued success. She had been raised with good manners and strong family values. She put me through a pre-game plan to meet her parents, and I followed it diligently. I thought the dinner went well; I followed all the etiquette rules, using the appropriate forks for each course. However, it became apparent that I hadn't impressed them enough. I fell short of their expectations for their daughter. The ironic part was that they treated her as if she weren't smart. She had done a few reckless and immature things before meeting me, which only reinforced their beliefs. However, I understood their reservations. As a college walk-on athlete from a broken home living alone in a city with few family members, it was difficult for them to see my drive to be the best version of myself. They were uncomfortable with my different views of the world and unsure about my influence on their daughter. Despite her parents' doubts, their daughter trusted her own heart more than their judgment. She had always been independent and somewhat rebellious as a teenager. Our love story unfolded, and the outcome of that meeting continues to thrive today. I proved to her skeptical parents that I would take care of their daughter better than they ever could. I would cherish her heart and encourage her to surpass their expectations. While it may have been another wrong reason for me to become successful, it was one that helped me beat the odds.

Impressing The Parents

Her father would often remind me that the "jury is still out on me." It was a legal expression, conveying his lack of trust and that he was keeping a close eye on me. Despite his words, he showed some support, and I treated him as if he were my biggest fan, valuing his approval. I reflected on his words, which affected my attitude quite a bit. I tried to act like it did not bother me, as I was going to prove my wife's family wrong. I was going to provide for her even better than they could. I was going to prove the true definition of love at first sight. My love overcame my desire to be accepted. I decided to be in love. When a person encounters me, they come into contact with love. My loves, you can live a life of love as well and stop trying to be accepted.

Yahweh (God) gave me a wife that accepted me for who I am, and I pray that you find that partner that accepts you in this life's journey while you walk the earth and helps complete your balanced life. God has preordained that person for you. If you are troubled and have a problem accepting life's twists and turns, use your God-given ability to access the Holy Spirit to calm your spirit and achieve balance. He will develop for you your own partner and team to trek this mission with you. You are at the front of the crowd, running in the Greatest Chase Ever. The blessing is that you also know what you are chasing.

Run on, my beloved.
Run on!

Conclusion

I HOPE THAT as you read my book, you had the opportunity to experience the joy of my romance with my wife, witness God's preservation of a man after a life of crime, and join me on my religious quest to find Yahweh and balance in my journey.

I would like to dedicate this book to my wife, Telisha Harris, my closest partner and friend. We have shared our entire adult lives together. I also dedicate it to my children, Martio Jr., Demari, Tomari, Martio 3rd, and daughter Jazzmyn. They have all been a great inspiration to me and have helped me maintain my balance. God has blessed me with a wonderful family instilled with good morals and values. I am also grateful for my mother, Marie V. Harris-Jones. She is courageous, bold, and never leans on her own understanding (well, sometimes—LOL).

I want to express my gratitude to all my friends and family who have had a relationship with me over the years. Each one of you has played a significant role in shaping me into the person I am today. I cherish every relationship and do not take any of them for granted. To my brothers and sisters in the faith, I walk with you and stand beside you. Balancing spiritual health with physical health is an art form that I have not yet mastered, but through following Christ, I have produced great work. I pray that my victories, triumphs, trials, and tribulations shared in this book will help readers navigate through their own trying times. To the spiritual individual, if you read this book, my experiences now belong to you. If I can be your Solomon, guiding you away from potential disaster, I hope this book brings blessings to your life.

www.ingramcontent.com/pod-product-compliance
Lightning Source LLC
Chambersburg PA
CBHW072016290426
44109CB00018B/2255